GRAMADEG CYMRAEG CYFOES
CONTEMPORARY WELSH GRAMMAR

Gramadeg Cymraeg Cyfoes

Contemporary Welsh Grammar

Paratowyd gan Uned Iaith Genedlaethol Cymru CBAC

Cyhoeddwyd gyntaf yn 1976 gan D. Brown a'i Feibion Cyf., Y Bont-faen.
Argraffiad newydd, yn cynnwys mân newidiadau, 1998
Ad-argraffiad 2000
Trydydd argraffiad 2003

ISBN 1 85902 672 9

ⓗ Uned Iaith Genedlaethol Cymru CBAC ©

Argraffwyd gan
Wasg Gomer, Llandysul, Ceredigion.

MYNEGAI - INDEX

THE ALPHABET

CONSONANTS

All consonants have one sound only in Welsh.

b	as in **b**oy
c	as in **c**at
ch	an aspirated "c" which does not occur in English. The sound is the same as the "ch" in lo**ch**.
d	as in **d**og
dd	as in **the**
f	as in o**f**
ff	as in o**ff**
g	as in **g**arden
ng	as in lo**ng**
h	as in **h**ang
j	as in **j**am
	There is no "k" in Welsh.
l	as in **l**adder
ll	an aspirated "l" which does not occur in English. It is very common in Welsh place names, e.g. **Ll**anelli.
m	as in **m**an
n	as in **n**ame
p	as in **p**et
ph	an aspirated "p" (pronounced as "ff"). It only occurs as a mutated form of "p", e.g. **p**en (head); ei **ph**en (her head).
	There is no "q" in Welsh.
r	as in **r**at
rh	an aspirated "r" which does not occur in English. The difference between "rh" and "r" is slight and is similar to the difference between "wh" and "w" e.g. **wh**en and **w**ent.
s	as in **s**ailor (except when followed by the vowel "i" when it is usually pronounced "sh", e.g. **si**op =**sh**op).
t	as in **t**own
tsh	as in **ch**ips
th	as in **th**ink
w	as in **w**ind
	("y" is not a consonant in Welsh)
	There is no "z" in Welsh (but the sound occurs with one or two borrowed words, e.g. "**sw**" (zoo) usually pronounced "zoo").

There are two consonants which are sometimes doubled in written Welsh. They are "n" and "r".

e.g. "n" tynnu (to pull); y ddannoedd (toothache).
"r" torri (to break, cut); gyrru (to drive, send).

These words must be learnt as they occur. Note that no other consonant in Welsh is doubled in any circumstances. ("Ll" and "ff" are not doubled letters but different sounds from "l" and "f").

The "f" at the end of words is not usually pronounced,

e.g. tref (pr. tre)   araf (pr. ara)

but it is not incorrect to pronounce the "f".

Some words end in a combination of consonants and a vowel may be interposed particularly in South Wales.

e.g. llyfr (pr. llyfyr)   cefn (pr. cefen)
llestr (pr. llester)   Note that the "r" in "ffenestr" is not pronounced.

It is, of course, not incorrect to pronounce these words without the vowel.

VOWELS

The vowels in Welsh are:
a, e, i, o, u, w, y
They may be long or short.

Long	*Short*
a as in gwlad (country) hard	mam (mother) ham
e as in hen (old) lane (as in Anglo Welsh dialect)	pren (wood) then
i as in hir (long) tree	inc (ink) pink
o as in to (roof) toe (as in Anglo Welsh dialect)	llon (happy) gone
w as in sw (zoo) zoo	lwc (luck) look
u as in un (one) been ⎱ These vowels have the	tun (tin) tin ⎱ These vowels
y as in dyn (man) seen ⎰ same sound.	cyn (before) pin ⎰ have the same sound.

In a relatively small number of words the circumflex accent (^) is used to denote long vowels:

e.g. môr   (sea)
pêl   (ball)
cân   (song)

It is important to learn these words as they arise.

In North Wales "y" and "u" in words of one syllable and in words which end in these sounds (e.g. gwely; canu) are pronounced slightly differently. (The sound is produced more in the throat).

Note the vowel "y".
It may be long as in "dyn" or short as in "cyn".

It has one sound in addition:

In "y(r)", "yn" and "fy" as "e" in the English word "the". In this instance it is a short vowel. Also in borrowed words, e.g. "nyrs".

In all words of one syllable except "y(r)", "yn" and "fy", the "y" is as in "dyn" or "cyn" etc.

In words of more than one syllable the sound "y" is the same as in "y(r)" and "fy" in all syllables except the *last* syllable.

In the last syllable it is the same as in "dyn", when no other letter follows, e.g. gwely (bed) (pr. gwelee); hynny (that) (pr. hynee); rheiny (those) (pr. rheinee).

In the last syllable it is the same as in "cyn", when followed by a consonant.

e.g. mynydd (mountain)   the first "y" is the same as in "y(r)", the second "y" is as in "cyn".

mynyddoedd (mountains) both "y's" are as in "y(r)" because neither occurs in the *last* syllable.

The diaeresis (¨) is sometimes used to denote that a vowel must be pronounced separately.

e.g. gweddïo   (to pray)
copïau   (copies)

Such words must be learnt as they occur.

DIPHTHONGS

ai	as in dail (leaves)	⎤ These all sound like the English "aye" except when
ae	as in Maesteg	they occur in final unaccentuated syllables, when
au	as in haul (sun)	they are pronounced "e" ("a" in certain parts of North Wales) e.g. cadeiriau--cadeirie.
aw	as in Penclawdd, as in the English word "away"	
eu	as in beudy (cowshed)	⎤ These are all pronounced like the word "eye" in
ei	as in Llandeilo	Anglo Welsh dialect.
ey	as in meysydd (fields)	
ew	as in Ceinewydd	
oe	as in Pencoed	⎤ These are all pronounced like "oy" in the English
oi	as in Llanboidy	"boy".
ou	as in cyffrous (exciting)	
ow	as in brown, as in the English "blow".	

iw   as in **lliw** (colour)
yw   as in **cyw** (chick)
uw   as in **Duw** (God)
wy   (i) as in **Gwyn**, as in the English "window".
        (ii) as in **Llwynypia**   There is no corresponding sound in English. It is rather similar to "**oy**" in "**boy**" but pronounced further forward on the lips.

> These are all pronounced like "ew" in the English Newport.

In some words the circumflex accent (^) is used to distinguish the sound. When the accent is placed above the ŵ the sound is as in Llwynypia.

e.g. gŵyl (festival)

When the accent is placed above the ŷ the sound is as in the English word "we".

e.g. gwŷr (husbands)

Words containing dipthongs which carry the circumflex accent have to be learnt as they arise.

ACCENTS

The accent is on the last syllable but one,
e.g. mýnydd; mynýddoedd
but there are some exceptions:
e.g. glanháu; paratói.

THE ARTICLE

The definite article ("the" in English) has three forms in Welsh:

1 "y" in front of consonants: e.g. y pentref (the village). Feminine singular nouns except for those beginning with "ll" and "rh" undergo soft mutation after 'y': e.g. tref, y dref (the town) but y llong (the ship), y rhaw (the shovel).

2 "yr" in front of vowels or "h": e.g. yr afon (the river), yr het (the hat).

3 "'r" after words ending in vowels: e.g. y ci a'r gath (the dog and the cat.)

Note that the "mae" followed by "y/yr" becomes "mae'r":

e.g. Mae'r plant ar y bws.   The children are on the bus.

In Welsh there is no indefinite article (a/an/any/some in English), therefore:

a book is "llyfr" (book)
an apple is "afal" (apple)
any money is "arian" (money)
some children is "plant" (children)

NOUNS

Nouns can be classified as either proper nouns (i.e. names of persons or places) or other nouns (i.e. normally words for things or objects). Here are some examples:

Proper Nouns: Gareth; Cymru (Wales); Mrs. Prys; Caerdydd (Cardiff).
Other Nouns: bachgen (boy); merch (girl); gwlad (country); tref (town).

Gender

In Welsh all nouns must be masculine or feminine. Unfortunately, there is no logical reason why some are masculine and others feminine.

e.g. drws (door) is masculine; ffenestr (window) is feminine.

Therefore it is important to learn the gender of the nouns as well as their meanings.

ADJECTIVES

The adjective generally comes after the noun in Welsh.

e.g. bachgen da   a good boy
     ci mawr   a big dog
     pentref bach   a small village

No mutation occurs after masculine singular nouns but adjectives preceded by feminine singular nouns take soft mutation.

e.g. merch dda   a good girl
     cath fawr   a large cat
     tref fach   a small town

Adjectives which follow plural nouns do not mutate, whether the nouns be masculine or feminine.

e.g. merched pert   pretty girls
     plant drwg   bad children

A few adjectives come before the noun and cause soft mutation.

e.g. **hen (old)**
     hen wraig   an old lady
     hen ddyn   an old man

prif (chief)
     prif reswm   chief reason

hoff (favourite)
    hoff wers   favourite lesson
    hoff raglen   favourite programme

unig (meaning "only")
    unig blentyn   only child
    unig ferch   only girl

(But when "unig" follows the adjective, it means "lonely" e.g. plentyn unig—lonely child).

ambell (some, a few, occasional)
    ambell waith   }
    ambell dro   sometimes

y fath (such)
    y fath le   such a place
    "Sut" is also used in this context in South Wales.
    e.g. sut le   such a place

The following adjectives also precede the noun but do not cause soft mutation.

rhai (some = a few)
    rhai pethau   a few things

peth (some = a small amount)
    peth llaeth   a small amount of milk

pob (every)
    pob dydd   every day

sawl (many, several)
    sawl bachgen   several boys

Gender

The feminine forms of adjectives in Welsh have largely disappeared from the spoken language but they are still used in certain combinations and only these need to be learnt.

    e.g. gafr wen   a white goat
         torth wen   a white loaf
         stori fer   a short story
         geneth fechan   a little girl
         y ford gron   the round table

Number

The plural forms of adjectives in Welsh have more or less disappeared from the spoken language.

e.g. bachgen mawr	a big boy
bechgyn mawr	big boys
siop newydd	a new shop
siopau newydd	new shops

Nevertheless, some plural forms are still used naturally and only these must be learnt.

e.g. pobl ifainc	young people
dynion eraill	other men

In some combinations plural forms, which have otherwise disappeared, are still used.

e.g. mwyar duon	blackberries
straeon byrion	short stories

COMPARISON OF ADJECTIVES

There are four degrees of comparison in Welsh: Positive, Equative, Comparative and Superlative.

(a) Regular Adjectives

Method 1. The most common method of comparing adjectives in Welsh is by placing mor . . . mwy . . . and mwya . . . in front of the adjective.

Positive	Equative	Comparative	Superlative
e.g. cryf	mor gryf	mwy cryf	mwya cryf
(strong)	(as/so strong)	(stronger)	(strongest)

Method 2. The following endings are added to the adjectives: -ed, -ach and -a/af. (The -f of this ending is frequently omitted leaving -a.)

Positive	Equative	Comparative	Superlative
e.g. cryf	cryfed	cryfach	cryfa
(strong)	(as/so strong)	(stronger)	(strongest)

Both of these different ways occur in speech and either the one form or the other can be used, but generally adjectives with more than two syllables always form their degrees of comparison by the first method.

(b) Irregular Adjectives

Positive	Equative	Comparative	Superlative
da (good)	mor dda	gwell	gorau
	cystal		

drwg (bad)	mor ddrwg	gwaeth	gwaetha
	cynddrwg		
mawr (big)	mor fawr	mwy	mwya
	cymaint		
bach (small)	mor fach	llai	lleia
	cyn lleied		
hen (old)	mor hen	henach	hena
ifanc (young)	mor ifanc	ifancach	ifanca
hawdd (easy)	mor hawdd	hawddach	hawdda
		mwy hawdd	mwya hawdd
anodd (difficult)	mor anodd	mwy anodd	mwya anodd
agos (near)	mor agos	agosach	agosa
hir (long)	mor hir	hirach	hira

Some of these adjectives now form their degrees of comparison like regular adjectives, but in literary Welsh they have irregular forms.

USES OF COMPARISON OF ADJECTIVES

1 Positive

(*a*) noun + adjective.

    e.g. llyfr gwyn   a white book
(But remember that certain adjectives are placed before the noun as explained earlier.)

(*b*) "yn" with soft mutation (except "ll" and "rh")+ adjective.

    e.g. Mae'r llyfr yn wyn.   The book is white.
         Mae'r botel yn llawn.   The bottle is full.

2 Equative (as . . . as)
(*a*)
Method 1.

"mor" with soft mutation of positive adjective (except "ll" and "rh") + "â" (with aspirate mutation of p, t, c)/"ag" (before vowels).

    e.g. Mae Alun mor dal â Siân.   Alun is as tall as Siân.
        Dydy'ch esgidiau chi ddim mor rhad   Your shoes are not as cheap as my shoes.
         â f'esgidiau i.
        Mae'i ffrog hi mor wyn ag eira.   Her dress is as white as snow.

Method 2.

"cyn" with soft mutation of equative adjective (except "ll" and "rh") + "â" (with aspirate mutation of p, t, c)/"ag" (before vowels).

14

e.g. Rydw i cyn gryfed â fe. — I'm as strong as he.

Ydy'r menyn yma cyn rhated â'r menyn yna? — Is this butter as cheap as that butter?

(b)

Adjectives in their equative degree may be used directly after the noun. No mutation occurs.

e.g. Dydw i ddim wedi gweld merch mor dal â hi o'r blaen. — I haven't seen a girl as tall as her before.

Oes chwaraewr cystal â chi yn y tîm? — Is there a player as good as you in the team?

Note

With the adjectives "da" (good), "drwg" (bad) and "mawr" (big), "cyn" no longer exists as a separate word and has become part of the equative degree.

e.g. Mae Siân cystal â Rhian. — Siân is as good as Rhian.

Mae'r ferch cynddrwg â'r bachgen. — The girl is as bad as the boy.

Mae ysgol Llanaber cymaint ag ysgol Llanarfon. — Llanaber school is as big as Llanarfon school.

3 Comparative (than)

(a)

Method 1.

"yn" with soft mutation of comparative adjective + "na" (with aspirate mutation of p, t, c)/"nag" (before vowels).

e.g. Mae e'n fwy tal na chi. — He is taller than you.

Mae hi'n fwy pert nag Elin. — She is prettier than Elin.

Similarly:

Mae e'n llai tal na chi. — He is less tall = shorter than you.

Mae hi'n llai pert nag Elin. — She is less pretty = uglier than Elin.

Method 2.

"yn" with soft mutation of comparative adjective (except "ll" and "rh") + "na" (with aspirate mutation of p, t, c)/"nag" (before vowels).

e.g. Mae e'n gryfach na chi. — He is stronger than you.

Mae Sbaeneg yn rhwyddach na Ffrangeg. — Spanish is easier than French.

Roedd y llyn yn ddyfnach na'r afon. — The lake was deeper than the river.

Mae e'n dalach nag Alun. — He's taller than Alun.

(b)

Adjectives in their comparative degree may be used directly after the noun and after feminine nouns soft mutation occurs.

e.g. Rydw i eisiau prynu cot fwy drud y tro nesa. — I want to buy a more expensive coat next time.

Dydw i ddim wedi gweld merch harddach erioed. — I have never seen a more beautiful girl.

Oes llyfr gwell gyda chi? — Have you got a better book?

4 Superlative (. . . est)

Since the adjective in the superlative degree either follows a definite noun or is used as a definite noun, the construction explained on Page 75 (2) must be used if the verb "Bod" (to be) is involved.

(a)

Method 1.

e.g. Hi ydy'r ferch fwya prydferth yn yr ysgol.   She is the most beautiful girl in the school.

(In this sentence the adjective follows the definite noun.)

Hi ydy'r fwya prydferth yn yr ysgol.   She is the most beautiful in the school.

(In this sentence the adjective is used as a definite noun and since the noun is feminine, soft mutation occurs.)

Method 2.

e.g. Fe oedd y bachgen tala yn y dosbarth.   He was the tallest boy in the class.
Fe ydy'r cryfa.   He's the strongest.

(b)

Adjectives in their superlative degree may be used directly after the noun and after feminine nouns soft mutation occurs.

e.g. Mae e wedi prynu'r car mwya drud.   He has bought the most expensive car.
Mae hi'n gwisgo'r ffrog fwya lliwgar.   She's wearing the most colourful dress.

Note

1 If the adjective in its positive form ends in -g, -b or -d, these letters harden to -c, -p and -t when the adjective is compared.

Positive	Equative	Comparative	Superlative
e.g. teg (fair)	teced (as/so fair)	tecach (fairer)	teca (fairest)
gwlyb (wet)	gwlyped (as/so wet)	gwlypach (wetter)	gwlypa (wettest)
drud (expensive)	druted (as/so expensive)	drutach (more expensive)	druta (most expensive)

Note also:

tlws (pretty)	tlysed (as/so pretty)	tlysach (prettier)	tlysa (prettiest)
trwm (heavy)	trymed (as/so heavy)	trymach (heavier)	tryma (heaviest)

2 Traditionally in literary Welsh and still in some dialects of spoken Welsh, "â/na" cause aspirate mutation.

1 Equative

Method 1

e.g. Roedd y bocs mor drwm a phlwm.   The box was as heavy as lead.

Method 2

e.g. Mae tocynnau'r plant cyn ddruted â   The children's tickets are as
thocynnau oedolion.   expensive as adults' tickets.

2 Comparative

Method 1

e.g. Roedd y dur yn pwyso'n fwy trwm na   The steel weighed heavier than three
thri bachgen.   boys.

Method 2

e.g. Mae tocynnau oedolion yn ddrutach   Adults' tickets are more expensive
na thocynnau'r plant.   than the children's.

This text book, however, follows the practice of dialects where the aspirate mutation after "â/na" is omitted.

3 When only two persons or things are compared, the comparative degree is used in English but the superlative degree must be used in Welsh.

e.g. Hi ydy'r fwya tlws o'r ddwy ferch.   She is the prettier of the two girls.

4 Adjectives in their positive, equative, comparative and superlative degrees can be used as adverbs.

e.g. *Positive*
Rhedodd e'n dda.   He ran well.

Equative
Mae e'n chwerthin mor uchel.   He laughs so loudly.

Comparative
Mae hi'n edrych yn henach.   She looks older.

Superlative
Nhw ganodd (yn) orau.   They sang best.

NUMERALS

Up to 10	*Masculine Forms*	*Feminine forms*
1	un	
2	dau	dwy
3	tri	tair
4	pedwar	pedair
5	pump	
6	chwech	
7	saith	
8	wyth	
9	naw	
10	deg	

The forms "pum" and "chwe" should be used when they come directly in front of a noun.

e.g. pum bachgen — five boys
chwe merch — six girls

Note also the use of "deng" as well as "deg" for 10 in the following combinations:
e.g. deng munud (ten minutes); deng mlynedd (ten years); deng mlwydd(oed) (ten years (of age)); deng mil (ten thousand); deng miliwn (ten million); deng modfedd (ten inches); deng milltir (ten miles).

Mutations

"Un" with soft mutation of feminine nouns except those beginning with "ll", "rh".

e.g. un ferch — one girl
un llaw — one hand

"Dau" with soft mutation of masculine nouns. "Dwy" with soft mutation of feminine nouns.

e.g. dau fachgen — two boys
dwy gath — two cats

In literary Welsh "tri" and "chwe" are followed by aspirate mutation, but this rule is generally broken in speech, except for a few notable exceptions:

e.g. tri chant (three hundred); chwe chant (six hundred); chwe cheiniog (sixpence); tri pheth (three things); tri phen (three heads/three pens).

After 10	*Masculine Forms*	*Feminine Forms*
11	un deg un	
12	un deg dau	un deg dwy
13	un deg tri	un deg tair
14	un deg pedwar	un deg pedair

After	Masculine forms	Feminine forms
20	dau ddeg	
21	dau ddeg un	
22	dau ddeg dau	dau ddeg dwy
30	tri deg	
31	tri deg un	
40	pedwar deg	
41	pedwar deg un	
50	pum deg/hanner cant	
51	pum deg un	
60	chwe deg	
100	cant	
1,000	mil, etc.	

The following pattern should be adopted when counting in Welsh:

(a) Up to 10,

Numeral + singular noun.

    e.g. saith ci   seven dogs

(b) After 10,

Numeral + "o" with soft mutation of plural forms.

    e.g. un deg tri o fechgyn   thirteen boys
         un deg tair o ferched   thirteen girls

         cant o lyfrau   a hundred books
         hanner cant o dai   fifty houses

But note the use of "can" in the following combinations:

can punt (a hundred pounds (£))
can pwys (a hundredweight)
can mlynedd (a hundred years)
can mlwyddiant (centenary)
can mil (a hundred thousand)
can miliwn (a hundred million)
can erw (a hundred acres)
can milltir (a hundred miles)
can tunnell (a hundred tons)

With the numbers 101 to 110 "a/ag" is used to link "cant" with the numerals 1 - 10.

    101   cant ag un
    109   cant a naw

Similarly.

209	dau gant a naw
406	pedwar cant a chwech
908	naw cant ag wyth

But when the number following the hundred exceeds 10, "a/ag" is not used.

119	cant un deg naw
517	pum cant un deg saith

Note that the numeral "un" (one) is not used before "cant" and "mil".

When stating the year in dates, there is no need to use the feminine forms of the numerals.

e.g. 1972   mil naw cant saith deg dau (or simply un naw saith dau)
      1853   mil wyth cant pum deg tri (un wyth pump tri)

Large numbers should be divided in this way:

17, 528, 130   un deg saith miliwn, pum cant dau ddeg wyth mil, cant tri deg.

"Dim" or "o" should be used when 0 is part of the telephone number.

2007   dau dim dim saith/dau "o" "o" saith.

Traditional Numerals

After 10	Masculine Forms	Feminine Forms
11	un ar ddeg	
12	deuddeg	
13	tri ar ddeg	tair ar ddeg
14	pedwar ar ddeg	pedair ar ddeg
15	pymtheg	
16	un ar bymtheg	
17	dau ar bymtheg	dwy ar bymtheg
18	deunaw	
19	pedwar ar bymtheg	pedair ar bymtheg
20	ugain	
21	un ar hugain	
22	dau ar hugain	dwy ar hugain
30	deg ar hugain	
31	un ar ddeg ar hugain	
32	deuddeg ar hugain	
40	deugain	
50	hanner cant	
60	trigain	
80	pedwar ugain	
100	cant	
1,000	mil	

etc.

Traditional numerals are used:

1 to tell the time

e.g. 12.00	deuddeg o'r gloch
8.40	ugain munud i naw
11.25	pum munud ar hugain wedi un ar ddeg

2 to tell one's age (especially up to 30)

e.g. 25 years old	pump ar hugain (mlwydd) oed
12 years old	deuddeg (mlwydd) oed

"Blwydd" can often be omitted.

ORDINALS

Up to 10	*Masculine Forms*	*Feminine Forms*
1st	cynta	
2nd	ail	
3rd	trydydd	trydedd
4th	pedwerydd	pedwaredd
5th	pumed	
6th	chweched	
7th	seithfed	
8th	wythfed	
9th	nawfed	
10th	degfed	

The use of the ordinal numbers up to 10

All ordinals except "cynta" are placed before the noun.

e.g. yr ail dŷ	the second house
y trydydd bachgen	the third boy
y nawfed llyfr	the ninth book

Note that "cynta" always follows the noun.

e.g. y dyn cynta	the first man
y bws cynta	the first bus
y wers gynta	the first lesson

Mutations

"Cynta": Soft mutation occurs in "cynta" when it is preceded by a feminine singular noun.

e.g. y ferch gynta   the first girl.

"Ail" with soft mutation of both masculine and feminine nouns.

e.g. yr ail fachgen   the second boy
     yr ail ferch   the second girl

Feminine ordinals take soft mutation after the article "y" and the nouns which they qualify also take soft mutation.

e.g. y drydedd waith   the third time
     y bedwaredd ysgol   the fourth school
     y bumed ferch   the fifth girl
     y ddegfed bennod   the tenth chapter

Masculine ordinals neither mutate themselves nor cause any mutation.

e.g. y trydydd bachgen   the third boy
     y pumed tŷ   the fifth house

After 10

The ordinals should be used in the following way:

e.g. the 11th boy   y bachgen un deg un
     the 67th hymn   yr emyn chwe deg saith

If in any doubt, the word "rhif" may be placed in front of the numeral, which then becomes an ordinal.

the 71st hymn   e.g. yr emyn rhif saith deg un
the 32nd boy   y bachgen rhif tri deg dau

When writing or referring to the date, the following pattern may be used:

e.g. July 15th   Gorffennaf un deg pump
     January 31st   Ionawr tri deg un

PRONOUNS

Personal Pronouns

In Welsh, personal pronouns are divided into two classes—independent (those which are not dependent on any other word in a sentence) and dependent (those which are dependent on another word in a sentence).

1 Independent

Singular		Plural	
(i) Simple			
1 fi (S.W.)	I, me	ni	we, us
mi (N.W.)			
2 ti	you	chi	you
3 fe/e (S.W.)	he, him		
fo/o (N.W.)		nhw	they, them
hi	she, her		

Singular		Plural	
(ii) Conjunctive			
1 finnau (S.W.)	I, me	ninnau	we, us
minnau (N.W.)			
2 tithau	you	chithau	you,
3 yntau	he, him	nhwthau	they, them
hithau	she, her		

The conjunctive pronouns convey a degree of emphasis. Learners need not use these pronouns but should be able to identify them.

2 Dependent

Prefixed forms

Singular		Plural	
1 fy, f', 'y (or merely the nasal mutation)	my	ein, 'n	our
2 dy, d'	your	eich, 'ch	your
3 ei, 'i, 'w (m)	his	eu, 'u, 'w	their
ei, 'i, 'w (f)	her		

Pronunciation: "ei" or "i"; "ein", "yn", or "n"; "eich", "ych" or "ch"; "eu" or "i" not the N.W. "u") are acceptable.

Affixed forms

Singular		Plural	
1 i (S.W.)		ni	
fi (N.W.)			
2 di, ti		chi	
3 e, fe (S.W.)		nhw	
o, fo (N.W.)			
hi			

Uses of the Independent Pronouns

1 As the direct object of a verb.

    e.g. Gwelais i nhw.   I saw them.
          Glywoch chi fi?   Did you hear me?

2 As the subject of a verb when the word order is inverted.

    e.g. Hi sy'n canu heno.   *She* is singing tonight.
          Fi sy'n gwybod orau.   *I* know best.

3 As the subject of the verb "Bod" when a definite noun or pronoun follows the verb.

    e.g. Fe oedd yr athro Cymraeg.   He was the Welsh teacher.
          Nhw ydy'r plant gorau.   They are the best children.

4 As a sentence equivalent in answering questions.

    e.g. Pwy oedd yn hwyr? Fi.   Who was late? I.
          Pwy fydd yn nofio yn y ras? Ni.   Who will be swimming in the race?
                                           We.

5 After certain prepositions which do not conjugate.

    e.g. Ewch gyda fe.   Go with him.
          Roedd hi'n eistedd gyferbyn â fi.   She was sitting opposite me.

6 After the conjunctions "a" (and), "na" (nor), "neu" (or), "ond" (but), "fel" (like), "mai" (that), "â" (as), "na" (than).

    e.g. Aeth Gareth a fi i weld y gêm.   Gareth and I went to see the game.

Note

The pronouns "fe" and "mi" are often used in speech before the inflected form of the verb as preverbial particles. When used in this way they have no meaning.

    e.g. Fe wela i chi.   I'll see you.
          Mi glywodd e.   He heard.
          Mi gysgais i yn y gadair.   I slept in the chair.
          Fe ddywedwn ni wrth yr athro.   We'll tell the teacher.

Uses of the Dependent Pronouns

Prefixed and Genitive forms ("fy", "f'", "y" etc.)

1 *Before nouns to denote possession.*

Dyma'ch llyfr chi.   This/Here is your book.
Rydw i a fy chwaer yn mynd i'r dref.   My sister and I are going to town.

2 *Before verb-nouns as equivalents of object pronouns.*

Roeddwn i eisiau ei gweld hi.	I wanted to see her.
Sut rydych chi'n f'adnabod i?	How do you know me?
Fyddwch chi'n dod gyda'ch ffrindiau?	Will you be coming with your friends?
Rydw i wedi'u clywed nhw o'r blaen.	I have heard them before.

Note that "ei" becomes "'i", "ein" becomes "'n", "eich" becomes "'ch" and "eu" becomes "'u" after words which end with a vowel.

e.g. a + ei	=	a'i		and his/her
â + ei	=	â'i		with his/her
gyda + eu	=	gyda'u		with their
dyma + eu	=	dyma'u		here are their

Similarly, after "tua" (towards), "â" (as), "na" (than), "o" (from), "wedi", etc.

Note that the genitive pronoun "'w" (third person singular or plural) is only used after the preposition "i" (to).

e.g. i'w dŷ e	to his house
i'w thŷ hi	to her house
i'w tŷ nhw	to their house

Affixed Pronouns

1 *After the personal forms of verbs and prepositions.*

Canais *i*.	I sang.
Weloch *chi*?	Did you see?
arni *hi*	on her/it
iddyn *nhw*	to them

2 *After nouns and verb-nouns when the prefixed pronoun has already been used.*

Ble mae dy gar *di*?	Where is your car?
Dyma'i chi *hi*.	Here is her dog.
Ydych chi wedi'u clywed *nhw*?	Have you heard them?
Mae e'n f'adnabod *i*.	He knows me.

The affixed pronoun is omitted if the same pronoun has been used immediately before it in the sentence.

e.g. Rydyn *ni*'n gwerthu'n car.	We are selling our car.

Note that the pronoun "ni" has already been used.

Note the following example—

Mae e wedi prynu'n car *ni*.	He has bought our car.

The pronoun is included since it has not been used previously in the sentence.

Mutations

"fy" + nasal mutation

e.g. pentref (village) fy mhentref i (my village)
     cath (cat) fy nghath i (my cat)

"dy" + soft mutation

e.g. tad (father) dy dad di (your father)
     mam (mother) dy fam di (your mother)

"ei"
"'i" } (m) + soft mutation
"'w"

e.g. llyfr (book) ei lyfr e (his book)
     tŷ (house) o'i dŷ e (from his house)
     cartref (home) i'w gartref e (to his home)

"ei"
"'i" } (f) + aspirate mutation
"'w"

e.g. pen (head) ei phen hi (her head)
     ci (dog) a'i chi hi (and her dog)
     teulu (family) i'w theulu hi (to her family)

In literary Welsh, words beginning with a vowel introduce the letter "h" after the following:

"ei"	(f) + noun/verb-noun	ei henw hi	her name
"'i"	(f) ,,	o'i hysgol hi	from her school
"'w"	(f) ,,	i'w heglwys hi	to her church
"ein"	,,	ein hateb ni	our answer
"eu"	,,	eu henwau nhw	their names
"'u"	,,	o'u heglwys nhw	from their church

This "h" is hardly discernible in speech.

Demonstrative Pronouns

y/yr/'r . . . yma   this   } In speech these tend to become "'ma", and "'na".
y/yr/'r . . . yna } that } "Acw" is pronounced as "'co" in South Wales.
y/yr/'r . . . acw }

e.g. y ferch yma   this girl   y dyn yma   this man
     y ferch yna } that girl   y dyn yna } that man
     y ferch acw }   y dyn acw }

These words are used to convey "this" and "that" in spoken Welsh with both masculine and feminine nouns.

They can also be used with plural nouns to convey "these" and "those".

e.g. y plant yma   these children

     y plant yna   }

     y plant acw   }   those children

In literary Welsh the following forms are used:

y/yr/'r . . . hwn	this (with masculine nouns)	y dyn hwn	this man
y/yr/'r . . . hwnnw	that ,,	y dyn hwnnw	that man
y/yr/'r . . . hon	this (with feminine nouns)	y ferch hon	this girl
y/yr/'r . . . honno	that ,,	y ferch honno	that girl
y/yr/'r . . . hyn	these (with plural nouns)	y plant hyn	these children
y/yr/'r . . . hynny	those ,,	y plant hynny	those children

"Hwn/hwnna" and "hon/honna" are used alone as pronouns when referring to persons or to tangible things.

e.g. Hwn/Hwnna ydy'r bachgen gorau yn y   This one/That one is the best boy in
     dosbarth.   the class.
     Hon/Honna ydy'r ferch fwya pert.   This one/That one is the prettiest girl.

The plural forms in this context are "y rhain" and "y rheina".

e.g. Mae'r rhain yn dda ond mae'r rheina'n   These are good but those are better.
     well.
     Dydw i ddim yn hoffi'r rhain.   I don't like these.
     Roedd y rheina'n ddrud.   Those were expensive.

"Hyn/hynny"' are used as pronouns when they refer to something abstract, such as news, events and sayings.

e.g. Glywoch chi hyn?   Did you hear this?
     Pryd digwyddodd hyn?   When did this happen?
     Weloch chi hynny?   Did you see that?
     Ble clywoch chi hynny?   Where did you hear that?

Reflexive Pronouns

"Self", "alone" and "own" are expressed in Welsh by placing the form "hun" or "hunan" (singular) and "hun" or "hunain" (plural) after the prefixed personal pronouns.

Singular	*Plural*
1 fy hun(an)	ein hun(ain)
2 dy hun(an)	eich hun(ain)
3 ei hun(an) (m)	eu hun(ain)
ei hun(an) (f)	

27

e.g. Rydw i'n gallu gweld fy hunan yn y   I can see myself in the mirror.
    drych.

    Maen nhw wedi lladd eu hunain.   They have killed themselves.

Note that in some words, the reflexive element is contained in the "ym" at the beginning of the word and the use of "fy hunan" etc. is incorrect.

e.g. ymolchi (to wash oneself)

    Rydw i'n ymolchi bob bore.   I wash myself every morning.

These pronouns can be used additionally as follows:

1 For emphasis with the meaning "self".

    e.g. Gwelais i'r pennaeth fy hunan.   I saw the headteacher myself.
        Maen nhw wedi talu eu hunain.   They have paid themselves.

2 For emphasis with the meaning "own".

    e.g. Brynoch chi'r llyfrau gyda'ch arian eich   Did you buy the books with your own
        hunain?   money?

    Des i gyda fy ffrindiau fy hunan.   I came with my own friends.

Note that in South Wales "wrth fy hunan" is commonly used with the meaning "on my own".

The idiom "ar fy mhen fy hunan" (S.W.) "ar fy mhen fy hun" (N.W.) is also used to convey the meaning "on my own", "alone".

RECIPROCAL PRONOUNS

Plural

1 gyda'n gilydd   together
2 gyda'ch gilydd   ,,
3 gyda'i gilydd   ,,

    e.g. Aethon nhw adre gyda'i gilydd.   They went home together.
        Ewch yna gyda'ch gilydd.   Go there together.
        Buon ni ar ein gwyliau gyda'n gilydd.   We went on our holidays together.

These are the only forms used.

Note that the singular pronoun "ei" is used in the third person plural, even when it refers to a plural noun or a third person plural pronoun.

    e.g. Aeth y plant i'r ysgol gyda'i gilydd.   The children went to school together.

THE VERB "BOD" TO BE

THE PRESENT TENSE

Affirmative

	Singular			Plural	
1	Rydw i	I am		Rydyn ni	We are
2	Rwyt ti	You are		Rydych chi	You are
3	Mae e/o	He is		Maen nhw	They are
	Mae hi	She is			

The pronouns "i, ti, e (S.W.)/o (N.W.), hi, ni, chi, nhw" always follow the personal forms of the verb, except when a noun follows the third person singular.

e.g. Mae Alun yn y tŷ.   Alun is in the house.
     Mae'r bechgyn yn yr ysgol.   The boys are in the school.

In the second person singular "Rwyt ti" is used when close friends talk to each other, parents speak to their children or people to their pets. In other instances "Rydych chi" is generally used.

Interrogative

	Singular			Plural	
1	Ydw i?	Am I?	Ydyn ni?	Are we?
2	Wyt ti?	Are you?	Ydych chi?	Are you?
3	Ydy e/o?	Is he?	Ydyn nhw?	Are they?
	Ydy hi?	Is she?		

Negative

	Singular			Plural	
1	Dydw i ddim	I am not	Dydyn ni ddim	We are not
2	Dwyt ti ddim	You are not	Dydych chi ddim	You are not
3	Dydy e/o ddim	He is not	Dydyn nhw ddim	They are not
	Dydy hi ddim	She is not		

Special Forms

Third person singular: "oes, sy"

Answer Forms

	Singular	Plural
	Yes/No	Yes/No
1	Ydw/Nag ydw	Ydyn/Nag ydyn
2	Wyt/Nag wyt	Ydych/Nag ydych
3	Ydy/Nag ydy	Ydyn/Nag ydyn
	Oes/Nag oes	

THE IMPERFECT TENSE

Affirmative

	Singular			Plural	
1	Roeddwn i	I was/used to	Roedden ni	We were/used to
2	Roeddet ti	You were/used to	Roeddech chi	You were/used to
3	Roedd e/o	He was/used to	Roedden nhw	They were/used to
	Roedd hi	She was/used to		

Interrogative

	Singular		Plural	
1	Oeddwn i?	Was I/Used I to?	Oedden ni?	Were we/Used we to?
2	Oeddet ti?	Were you/Used you to?	Oeddech chi?	Were you/Used you to?
3	Oedd e/o?	Was he/Used he to?	Oedden nhw?	Were they/Use they to?
	Oedd hi?	Was she/Used she to?		

Negative

	Singular			Plural	
1	Doeddwn i ddim	I wasn't/I used not to		Doedden ni ddim	We weren't
2	Doeddet ti ddim	You weren't	etc.	Doeddech chi ddim	You weren't
3	Doedd e/o ddim	He wasn't		Doedden nhw ddim	They weren't
	Doedd hi ddim	She wasn't			

Answer Forms

	Singular Yes/No	Plural Yes/No
1	Oeddwn/Nag oeddwn	Oedden/Nag oedden
2	Oeddet/Nag oeddet	Oeddech/Nag oeddech
3	Oedd/Nag oedd	Oedden/Nag oedden

Before all the tenses of the verb "Bod" listed below, the particles "fe"/"mi", both of which cause soft mutation, may be used. However these particles cannot be used with the tenses listed above.

THE FUTURE TENSE

Affirmative

	Singular			Plural	
1	Bydda i	I shall be	Byddwn ni	We shall be
2	Byddi di	You will be	Byddwch chi	You will be
3	Bydd e/o	He will be	Byddan nhw	They will be
	Bydd hi	She will be		

Interrogative

	Singular			Plural	
1	Fydda i?	Shall I be?	Fyddwn ni?	Shall we be?
2	Fyddi di?	Will you be?	Fyddwch chi?	Will you be?
3	Fydd e/o?	Will he be?	Fyddan nhw?	Will they be?
	Fydd hi?	Will she be?		

Negative

	Singular			Plural	
1	Fydda i ddim	I shall not be	Fyddwn ni ddim	We shall not be
2	Fyddi di ddim	You will not be	Fyddwch chi ddim	You will not be
3	Fydd e/o ddim	He will not be	Fyddan nhw ddim	They will not be
	Fydd hi ddim	She will not be		

Answer Forms

	Singular	Plural
	Yes/No	Yes/No
1	Bydda/Na fydda	Byddwn/Na fyddwn
2	Byddi/Na fyddi	Byddwch/Na fyddwch
3	Bydd/Na fydd	Byddan/Na fyddan

THE PAST TENSE

Affirmative

	Singular			Plural	
1	Bues i	I was	Buon ni	We were
2	Buest ti	You were	Buoch chi	You were
3	Buodd e/o	He was	Buon nhw	They were
	Buodd hi	She was		

Interrogative

	Singular			Plural	
1	Fues i?	Was I?	Fuon ni?	Were we?
2	Fuest ti?	Were you?	Fuoch chi?	Were you?
3	Fuodd e/o?	Was he?	Fuon nhw?	Were they?
	Fuodd hi?	Was she?		

Negative

	Singular			Plural	
1	Fues i ddim	I wasn't	Fuon ni ddim	We weren't
2	Fuest ti ddim	You weren't	Fuoch chi ddim	You weren't
3	Fuodd e/o ddim	He wasn't	Fuon nhw ddim	They weren't
	Fuodd hi ddim	She wasn't		

Answer Forms
Note

Do (Yes), Naddo (No).

"Bues i" etc. can be used to express the following meanings.

1 Bues i yng Nghaerdydd ddoe.	⎰ I was in Cardiff yesterday. ⎱ I went to Cardiff yesterday.
2 Bues i'n dysgu nofio yn y parc.	I learnt to swim in the park.

This does not have the same meaning as the Past Tense (e.g. Dysgais i nofio yn y parc) since it implies that the action was a continuous one until eventually completed. If learners find this concept difficult to comprehend, they will find that at this stage in their learning the Imperfect Tense will suffice.

THE CONDITIONAL TENSE

Affirmative

Singular		Plural	
1 Baswn i	I would (be)	Basen ni	We would (be)
2 Baset ti	You would (be)	Basech chi	You would (be)
3 Basai fe/fo	He would (be)	Basen nhw	They would (be)
Basai hi	She would (be)		

Interrogative

Singular		Plural	
1 Faswn i?	Would I (be)?	Fasen ni?	Would we (be)?
2 Faset ti?	Would you (be)?	Fasech chi?	Would you (be)?
3 Fasai fe/fo?	Would he (be)?	Fasen nhw?	Would they (be)?
Fasai hi?	Would she (be)?		

Negative

Singular		Plural	
1 Faswn i ddim	I would not (be)	Fasen ni ddim	We would not (be)
2 Faset ti ddim	You would not (be)	Fasech chi ddim	You would not (be)
3 Fasai fe/fo ddim	He would not (be)	Fasen nhw ddim	They would not (be)
Fasai hi ddim	She would not (be)		

Answer Forms

Singular Yes/No	Plural Yes/No
1 Baswn/Na faswn	Basen/Na fasen
2 Baset/Na faset	Basech/Na fasech
3 Basai/Na fasai	Basen/Na fasen

Alternative form of this tense

Affirmative

	Singular			*Plural*	
1	Byddwn i	I would (be)	Bydden ni	We would (be)
2	Byddet ti	You would (be)	Byddech chi	You would (be)
3	Byddai fe/fo	He would (be)	Bydden nhw	They would (be)
	Byddai hi	She would (be)		

Interrogative

	Singular			*Plural*	
1	Fyddwn i?	Would I (be)?	Fydden ni?	Would we (be)?
2	Fyddet ti?	Would you (be)?	Fyddech chi?	Would you (be)?
3	Fyddai fe/fo?	Would he (be)?	Fydden nhw?	Would they (be)?
	Fyddai hi?	Would she (be)?		

Negative

	Singular			*Plural*	
1	Fyddwn i ddim	I would not (be)	Fydden ni ddim	We would not (be)
2	Fyddet ti ddim	You would not (be)	Fyddech chi ddim	You would not (be)
3	Fyddai fe/fo ddim	He would not (be)	Fydden nhw ddim	They would not (be)
	Fyddai hi ddim	She would not (be)		

Answer Forms

	Singular Yes/No	*Plural* Yes/No
1	Byddwn/Na fyddwn	Bydden/Na fydden
2	Byddet/Na fyddet	Byddech/Na fyddech
3	Byddai/Na fyddai	Bydden/Na fydden

"Baswn i" etc. is given priority. This form is used in the courses prepared by the National Language Unit.

THE SUBJUNCTIVE CONDITIONAL TENSE

Affirmative

	Singular			*Plural*	
1	Pe baswn i	If I were (to)	Pe basen ni	If we were (to)
2	Pe baset ti	If you were (to)	Pe basech chi	If you were (to)
3	Pe basai fe/fo	If he were (to)	Pe basen nhw	If they were (to)
	Pe basai hi	If she were (to)		

Negative

	Singular			*Plural*	
1	Pe baswn i ddim	If I weren't (to)	Pe basen ni ddim	If we weren't (to)
2	Pe baset ti ddim	If you weren't (to)	Pe basech chi ddim	If you weren't (to)
3	Pe basai fe/fo ddim	If he weren't (to)	Pe basen nhw ddim	If they weren't (to)
	Pe basai hi ddim	If she weren't (to)		

Alternative form of this tense

Affirmative

	Singular		Plural
1 Pe bawn i	If I were (to)	Pe baen ni	If we were (to)
2 Pe baet ti	If you were (to)	Pe baech chi	If you were (to)
3 Pe bai e/o	If he were (to)	Pe baen nhw	If they were (to)
Pe bai hi	If she were (to)		

Negative

	Singular		Plural
1 Pe bawn i ddim	If I weren't (to)	Pe baen ni ddim	If we weren't (to)
2 Pe baet ti ddim	If you weren't (to)	Pe baech chi ddim	If you weren't (to)
3 Pe bai e/o ddim	If he weren't (to)	Pe baen nhw ddim	If they weren't (to)
Pe bai hi ddim	If she weren't (to)		

Note that with the negative forms no soft mutation occurs.

"Pe baswn i ddim", etc.
"Pe bawn i ddim", etc.

THE REGULAR VERB e.g. CANU—TO SING

The tenses of the regular verb are formed by using the verb "Bod" (to be) as an auxiliary, apart from the following inflected tenses (i.e. tenses which have their own endings). The endings are added to the stem of the verbs. (See page 39).

THE PAST TENSE

	Singular		Plural
1 Canais i	I sang	Canon ni	We sang
2 Canaist ti	You sang	Canoch chi	You sang
3 Canodd e/o	He sang	Canon nhw	They sang
Canodd hi	She sang		

THE FUTURE TENSE

	Singular		Plural
1 Cana i	I shall/will sing	Canwn ni	We shall/will sing
2 Cani di	You will sing	Canwch chi	You will sing
3 Caniff/Canith e/o	He will sing	Canan nhw	They will sing
Caniff/Canith hi	She will sing		

THE CONDITIONAL TENSE

	Singular		*Plural*
1 Canwn i	I would sing	Canen ni	We would sing
2 Canet ti	You would sing	Canech chi	You would sing
3 Canai fe/fo	He would sing	Canen nhw	They would sing
Canai hi	She would sing		

THE PRESENT TENSE

The Present Tense is formed by using the verb "Bod" ("Rydw i" . . . etc.) followed by "yn" and "canu". This gives both meanings of the Present Tense forms in English.

e.g. Mae Gareth yn canu.
1 Gareth is singing.
2 Gareth sings.

Similarly:
Mae Gareth yn mynd.
1 Gareth is going.
2 Gareth goes.

The "yn" is usually abbreviated to " 'n" when it follows a word ending in a vowel.

e.g. Rydw i'n ymolchi.
I am washing.
I wash.

Further examples

Rydw i'n chwarae.	I am playing.
Mae'r plant yn rhedeg.	The children are running.
Dydyn nhw ddim yn dod.	They aren't coming.
Ydych chi'n siarad Cymraeg?	Do you speak Welsh?
Ydy'r dyn yn gyrru?	Is the man driving?
Dydyn ni ddim yn addo.	We aren't promising.

In North Wales this Habitual Present Tense is conveyed by using "Bydda i", etc. (See page 32).

THE PAST TENSE

This tense is formed by adding the endings "-ais, -aist, -odd, -on, -och, -on" to the stem of the verb-noun. It is used to convey a completed action in the past.

e.g. Canais i.
I sang.

Further Examples

Rhedais i i'r ysgol y bore yma.	I ran to school this morning.
Bwyton nhw'r cinio i gyd.	They ate all the dinner.
Gofioch chi'r llyfr?	Did you remember the book?
Sgrechiodd hi?	Did she scream?
Ddihangais i ddim.	I didn't escape.
Ddechreuais i ddim am saith o'r gloch.	I didn't start at seven o'clock.

Verbs that begin with p, t, c, undergo aspirate mutation in their negative forms. This has been caused by the negative particle "ni" which no longer has to be written.

e.g. P   >   Ph   prynu (to buy)   Phrynais i ddim.   I didn't buy.
     T   >   Th   talu (to pay)   Thalais i ddim.   I didn't pay.
     C   >   Ch   cerdded (to walk)   Cherddais i ddim.   I didn't walk.

Verbs that begin with b, d, g, ll, m, rh, undergo soft mutation in their negative forms.

e.g. B   >   F   boddi (to drown)   Foddais i ddim.   I didn't drown.
     D   >   Dd   dysgu (to teach/learn) Ddysgais i ddim.   I didn't teach/learn.
     G   >   —   gyrru (to drive)   Yrrais i ddim.   I didn't drive.
     Ll   >   L   llithro (to slip)   Lithrais i ddim.   I didn't slip.
     M   >   F   methu (to fail)   Fethais i ddim.   I didn't fail.
     Rh   >   R   rhwyfo (to row)   Rwyfais i ddim.   I didn't row.

An indefinite object takes soft mutation after the affirmative and interrogative forms.

e.g. Welais i ferch ar y stryd?   Did I see a girl on the street?
     Clywais i fachgen yn gweiddi.   I heard a boy shouting.
     Darllenais i lyfrau da yn y llyfrgell.   I read some good books in the library.

But there is no mutation in the negative.

e.g. Ches i ddim cinio.   I didn't have any dinner.
     Yfais i ddim te.   I didn't drink any tea.
     Ddarllenais i ddim llyfrau.   I didn't read any books.

When the object is definite and preceded by the article, the mutation rules governing the noun are the same as those set out under **The Article**. (See page 12).

In the negative, the definite object is preceded by "mo" (ddim o) with proper nouns and "mo'r" (ddim o'r) with other nouns.

e.g. Welais i mo John/Siân.   I didn't see John/Siân.
     Welais i mo'r bachgen/ferch/plant.   I didn't see the boy/girl/children.

"Mo" is a contraction of "ddim o". It changes to "ddim ohono i, ddim ohono fe/hi" etc., when followed by a pronoun. This, in its contracted form, becomes "mono i, mono fe, moni hi" etc. For the full declension see page 56.

e.g. Welais i mono fe.   I didn't see him.
     Welon nhw monon ni.   They didn't see us.

STEMS OF VERB-NOUNS

1 The stem usually consists of that part of the verb-noun which remains when the ending drops.

e.g.			
-u	can-u	can-ais i	I sang
-i	cod-i	cod-ais i	I rose/got up
-ed	cerdd-ed	cerdd-ais i	I walked
-eg	rhed-eg	rhed-ais i	I ran
-a	bwyt-a	bwyt-ais i	I ate
-o	eglur-o	eglur-ais i	I explained
-yd	dychwel-yd	dychwel-ais i	I returned
-ig	ared-ig	ared-ais i	I ploughed
-yll	sef-yll	sef-ais i	I stood

Note that the **i** in the verb-noun endings "-io, -ian" is retained in the stem.

e.g.			
-o	cofi-o	cofi-ais	I remembered
-an	sgrechi-an	sgrechi-ais i	I shrieked

2 With some verbs the stem is the same as the verb-noun and the endings "-ais, -aist, -odd, -on, -och, -on" are added directly to them, e.g.

eistedd	eistedd-ais i	I sat
deall	deall-ais i	I understood
dangos	dangos-ais i	I showed
darllen	darllen-ais i	I read
chwerthin	chwerthin-ais i	I laughed
cadw	cadw-ais i	I kept
cyfaddef	cyfaddef-ais i	I admitted

The Past Tense of the following verbs are formed in the same way except for some additional changes.

addo	addaw-ais i	I promised
gwrando	gwrandaw-ais i	I listened
aros	arhos-ais i	I waited/stayed/stopped
cynnwys	cynhwys-ais i	I contained/included
cyrraedd	cyrhaedd-ais i	I reached/arrived
cynnal	cynhal-iais i	I held/supported
atal	atal-iais i	I stopped
bwrw	bwr-iais i	I threw
trin	trin-iais i	I treated
disgwyl	disgwyl-iais i	I expected
newid	newid-iais i	I changed
caniatáu	caniateu-ais i	I allowed
casáu	caseu-ais i	I hated
dadlau	dadleu-ais i	I argued
dechrau	dechreu-ais i	I started

derbyn	derbyn-iais i	I received
glanhau	glanheu-ais i	I cleaned
llawenhau	llawenheu-ais i	I rejoiced
mwynhau	mwynheu-ais i	I enjoyed
nesáu	neseu-ais i	I approached
parhau (para)	parheu-ais i	I continued
gwau	gweu-ais i	I knitted
hau	heu-ais i	I sowed
amau	amheu-ais i	I doubted
cynnau	cynheu-ais i	I lit
cau	cae-ais i	I closed
arwain	arwein-iais i	I led
bygwth	bygyth-iais i	I threatened
meddwl	meddyl-iais i	I thought
sibrwd	sibryd-ais i	I whispered
cyffwrdd (â)	cyffyrdd-ais i (â)	I touched
gweld	gwel-ais i	I saw
ymweld (â)	ymwel-ais i (â)	I visited
dianc	dihang-ais i	I escaped
dwyn	dyg-ais i	I stole
gadael	gadaw-ais i	I left/allowed
ymdael (â)	ymadaw-ais i (â)	I departed
dweud	dywed-ais i	I said

3 Some verbs are irregular:

bod	bues i	I was
mynd	es i	I went
dod	des i	I came
cael	ces i	I had
gwneud	gwnes i	I did/made
adnabod	adnabydd-ais i	I knew
canfod	canfydd-ais i	I perceived
cyfarfod	cyfarfydd-ais i	I met
darganfod	darganfydd-ais i	I discovered

THE PERFECT TENSE

This tense is formed by using the Present Tense of the verb "Bod" ("Rydw i" . . . etc.) followed by "wedi" and "canu".

e.g. Mae e wedi canu.　　　　He has sung.

Similarly:

Dydych chi ddim wedi byhafio.　　You haven't behaved.
Ydyn nhw wedi cyrraedd?　　Have they arrived?

THE PERFECT CONTINUOUS TENSE

This tense is formed by using the Present Tense of the verb "Bod" ("Rydw i" . . . etc.) followed by "wedi bod yn" and "canu".

e.g. Mae hi wedi bod yn canu.	She has been singing.

Similarly:

Rydw i wedi bod yn chwarae.	I have been playing.
Rwyt ti wedi bod yn gweithio.	You have been working.
Ydy e wedi bod yn cysgu?	Has he been sleeping?
Dydw i ddim wedi bod yn dysgu.	I haven't been teaching/learning.

THE IMPERFECT TENSE

This tense is formed by using the Imperfect Tense of the verb "Bod" ("Roeddwn i" . . . etc.) followed by "yn" and "canu".

It conveys the following meanings in English:

1 Roeddwn i'n canu ar y pryd.	I was singing at the time.
2 Roedd e'n canu yn y côr.	He used to sing in the choir.

Similarly:

Roedden nhw'n byw yn Llantrisant.	They used to live in Llantrisant.
Oedd e'n rhedeg yn y ras llynedd?	Was he running in the race last year?
Doeddech chi ddim yn darllen neithiwr.	You weren't reading last night.

The second usage of "Roedd . ." is confined to South Wales. If the repetitive nature of the act needs to be emphasised, "yn arfer" is used.

e.g. Roedd e'n arfer mynd i'r gwaith ar y bws.	He used to go to work on the bus.

This second meaning is conveyed in North Wales by using the alternative form of the Conditional Tense ("Byddwn i" . . . etc.). For the full declension of this tense, see page 35.

e.g. Byddwn i'n mynd i'r ysgol ar y bws.	I used to go to school on the bus.

THE PLUPERFECT TENSE

This tense is formed by using the Imperfect Tense of the verb "Bod" ("Roeddwn i" . . . etc.) followed by "wedi" and "canu".

e.g. Roeddwn i wedi canu.	I had sung.

Similarly:

Roedden nhw wedi penderfynu.	They had decided.
Doeddwn i ddim wedi pwdu.	I hadn't sulked.
Oeddech chi wedi ceisio/trio?	Had you tried?

THE PLUPERFECT CONTINUOUS TENSE

This tense is formed by using the Imperfect Tense of the verb "Bod" ("Roeddwn i" ... etc.) followed by "wedi bod yn" and "canu".

e.g. Roeddwn i wedi bod yn canu.   I had been singing.

Similarly:

Roedd y ferch wedi bod yn nofio.	The girl had been swimming.
Doedd e ddim wedi bod yn wylo.	He hadn't been crying.
Oedd y bachgen wedi bod yn ymladd?	Had the boy been fighting?

THE FUTURE TENSE (1)

This tense is formed by using the Future Tense of the verb "Bod" ("Bydda i" ...etc.) followed by "yn" and "canu".

It conveys the English meaning "I shall/will be . . ." etc.

e.g. Bydda i'n canu yfory.   I will be singing tomorrow.

Similarly:

Byddwn ni'n siopa yn y dref.	We shall be shopping in the town.
Fydd e ddim yn gyrru.	He will not (won't) be driving.

Note that in North Wales this tense also conveys **one** meaning of the Present Tense (see page 37).

e.g. Bydda i'n rhedeg bob bore.   I *run* every morning.

THE FUTURE PERFECT TENSE

This tense is formed by using the Future Tense of the verb "Bod" ("Bydda i" ... etc.) followed by "wedi" and "canu".

It conveys the English meaning "I shall/will have" . . . etc.

e.g. Bydda i wedi canu erbyn saith o'r gloch. I will have sung by seven o'clock.

Similarly:

Bydd e wedi gorffen mewn pum munud.	He will have finished in five minutes.
Fyddan nhw wedi paratoi popeth?	Will they have prepared everything?

THE FUTURE PERFECT CONTINUOUS TENSE

This tense is formed by using the Future Tense of the verb "Bod" ("Bydda i" ... etc.) followed by "wedi bod yn" and "canu".

It conveys the English meaning "I shall/will have been . . ." etc.

e.g. Bydda i wedi bod yn canu gyda'r grŵp am ddwy flynedd cyn bo hir.

I will have been singing with the group for two years before long.

Similarly:

Bydd hi wedi bod yn nofio drwy'r prynhawn.

She will have been swimming throughout the afternoon.

Fyddwch chi wedi bod yn gwersylla cyn diwedd y mis?

Will you have been camping before the end of the month?

THE FUTURE TENSE (2)

This tense is formed by adding the endings "-a, -i, -ith/-iff, -wn, -wch, -an" to the stem of the verb-noun (see page 39). It is used to convey the English meaning "I shall/will" ... etc.

e.g. Cana i.   I shall/will sing.

Irregular verbs are declined in full on pages 44-48.

With the verbs "gallu" and "medru" (to be able) this tense conveys the Present rather than the Future meaning.

e.g. Fedrwch chi weld?   Can you see?
     Allan nhw ddod gyda ni?   Can they come with us?

See also the verb "gwybod" (to know), page 47.

THE CONDITIONAL TENSE

Apart from the verbs "hoffi", "gallu" and "medru" which are conjugated regularly (e.g. "hoffwn i", etc.), and "gwybod" ("gwyddwn i", etc.), you need not concern yourselves with the short form of the Conditional Tense, but you should be prepared to identify it.

This tense is generally conveyed by using the Conditional Tense of the verb "Bod" ("Baswn i" ... etc.) followed by "yn" and "canu". It is used to express the meaning "I would" etc. and "I would be" etc. in English.

e.g. Baswn i'n canu.   I would sing/I would be singing.
     Basai fe'n chwarae.   He would play.
     Baswn i'n gweithio.   I would be working.

THE PERFECT CONDITIONAL TENSE

This tense is formed by using the Conditional Tense of the verb "Bod" ("Baswn i" ... etc.) followed by "wedi" and "canu". It conveys the English meaning "I would have" ... etc.

e.g. Baswn i wedi canu.   I would have sung.
     Fasai fe ddim wedi dod.   He wouldn't have come.
     Fasech chi wedi gofyn?   Would you have asked?

THE PERFECT CONDITIONAL CONTINUOUS TENSE

This tense is formed by using the Conditional Tense of the verb "Bod" ("Baswn i" . . . etc.) followed by "wedi bod yn" and "canu". It conveys the English meaning "I would have been" . . . etc.)

e.g. Baswn i wedi bod yn canu.	I would have been singing.
Fasai fe wedi bod yn gyrru?	Would he have been driving?
Fasai hi ddim wedi bod yn siopa yn y prynhawn.	She wouldn't have been shopping in the afternoon.

(Note the Subjunctive forms of the Conditional Tense:

e.g. Pe baswn i'n canu . . .	If I were singing/to sing . . .
Pe basen nhw wedi canu . . .	If they had sung . . .
Pe basai hi ddim wedi bod yn canu . . .	If she hadn't been singing . . .

IRREGULAR VERBS

THE VERB "MYND"—TO GO

The Future Tense (2)

	Singular		Plural
1 Â/Af i	I shall go	Awn ni	We shall go
2 Ei di	You will go	Ewch chi	You will go
3 Aiff/Eith e/o	He will go	Ân nhw	They will go
Aiff/Eith hi	She will go		

The Imperative

Dos/Cer (sing) ⎱	
Ewch/cerwch (pl.) ⎰	Go
Gadewch i ni fynd	Let us go, etc.

The Conditional Tense

	Singular		Plural
1 Awn (Elwn) i	I would go	Aen (Elen) ni	We would go
2 Aet (Elet) ti	You would go	Aech (Elech) chi	You would go
3 Âi e/o (Elai fe)	He would go	Aen (Elen) nhw	They would go
Âi (Elai) hi	She would go		

The Past Tense

	Singular		Plural
1 Es i	I went	Aethon ni	We went
2 Est ti	You went	Aethoch chi	You went
3 Aeth e/o	He went	Aethon nhw	They went
Aeth hi	She went		

THE VERB "DOD"—TO COME

The Future Tense (2)

	Singular			Plural	
1	Do/Dof i	I shall come	Down ni		We shall come
2	Doi di	You will come	Dewch chi		You will come
3	Daw e/o	He will come	Dôn nhw		They will come
	Daw hi	She will come			

The Imperative

Tyrd/Dere (sing)
Dowch/Dewch (pl.) } Come

Gadewch i ni ddod   Let us come, etc.

The Conditional Tense

	Singular		Plural	
1	Down (Delwn) i	I would come	Doen (Delen) ni	We would come
2	Doet (Delet) ti	You would come	Doech (Delech) chi	You would come
3	Dôi e/o (Delai fe)	He would come	Doen (Delen) nhw	They would come
	Dôi (Delai) hi	She would come		

The Past Tense

	Singular		Plural	
1	Des i	I came	Daethon ni	We came
2	Dest ti	You came	Daethoch chi	You came
3	Daeth e/o	He came	Daethon nhw	They came
	Daeth hi	She came		

THE VERB "GWNEUD"—TO DO/MAKE

The Future Tense (2)

	Singular		Plural	
1	Gwna/Gwnaf i	I shall do/make	Gwnawn ni	We shall do/make
2	Gwnei di	You will do/make	Gwnewch chi	You will do/make
3	Gwnaiff/Gwneith e/o	He will do/make	Gwnân nhw	They will do/make
	Gwnaiff/Gwneith hi	She will do/make		

The Imperative

Gwna (sing)
Gwnewch (pl.) } Do/make

Gadewch i ni wneud   Let us do/make, etc.

The Conditional Tense

Singular		Plural	
1 Gwnawn (Gwnelwn) i	I would do/make	Gwnaen (Gwnelen) ni	We would do/make
2 Gwnaet (Gwnelet) ti	You would do/make	Gwnaech (Gwnelech) chi	You would do/make
3 Gwnâi e/o (Gwnelai fe)	He would do/make	Gwnaen (Gwnelen) nhw	They would do/make
Gwnâi (Gwnelai) hi	She would do/make		

The Past Tense

Singular		Plural	
1 Gwnes i	I did/made	Gwnaethon ni	We did/made
2 Gwnest ti	You did/made	Gwnaethoch chi	You did/made
3 Gwnaeth e/o	He did/made	Gwnaethon nhw	They did/made
Gwnaeth hi	She did/made		

THE VERB "CAEL"—TO HAVE

The Future Tense (2)

Singular		Plural	
1 Ca/Caf i	I shall have	Cawn ni	We shall have
2 Cei di	You will have	Cewch chi	You will have
3 Caiff/Ceith e/o	He will have	Cân nhw	They will have
Caiff/Ceith hi	She will have		

The Imperative

Gadewch i ni gael   Let us have, etc.

The Imperative form in the second person is expressed by "cymera" (sing.) and "cymerwch" (pl.) = take. "Hwre" (sing.) and "hwrwch" (pl.) are widely used in S. Wales (when the action involves the passing of a particular object from hand to hand).

The Conditional Tense

Singular		Plural	
1 Cawn (Celwn) i	I would have	Caen (Celen) ni	We would have
2 Caet (Celet) ti	You would have	Caech (Celech) chi	You would have
3 Câi e/o (Celai fe)	He would have	Caen (Celen) nhw	They would have
Câi (Celai) hi	She would have		

The Past Tense

Singular		Plural	
1 Ces i	I had	Cawson ni	We had
2 Cest ti	You had	Cawsoch chi	You had
3 Cafodd e/o	He had	Cawson nhw	They had
Cafodd hi	She had		

THE VERB "ADNABOD" (NABOD)—TO KNOW (A PERSON)/RECOGNISE

The Future Tense (2)

	Singular		Plural	
1	Adnabydda/ Adnabyddaf i	I shall know	Adnabyddwn ni	We shall know
2	Adnabyddi di	You will know	Adnabyddwch chi	You will know
3	Adnabyddiff/ Adnabyddith e/o	He will know	Adnabyddan nhw	They will know
	Adnabyddiff/ Adnabyddith hi	She will know		

The Conditional Tense

	Singular		Plural	
1	Adnabyddwn i	I would know	Adnabydden ni	We would know
2	Adnabyddet ti	You would know	Adnabyddech chi	You would know
3	Adnabyddai fe/fo	He would know	Adnabydden nhw	They would know
	Adnabyddai hi	She would know		

The Past Tense

	Singular		Plural	
1	Adnabyddais i	I knew	Adnabyddon ni	We knew
2	Adnabyddaist ti	You knew	Adnabyddoch chi	You knew
3	Adnabyddodd e/o	He knew	Adnabyddon nhw	They knew
	Adnabyddodd hi	She knew		

Similarly:

Cyfarfod (â)	to meet
Cydnabod	to acknowledge
Darfod	to finish
Canfod	to see, perceive
Darganfod	to discover

THE VERB "GWYBOD"—TO KNOW (A FACT)

The Present Tense

Unlike most other verbs "Gwn i" etc. conveys the Present rather than the Future Tense.

	Singular		Plural	
1	Gwn i	I know	Gwyddon ni	We know
2	Gwyddost ti	You know	Gwyddoch chi	You know
3	Gŵyr e/o	He knows	Gwyddan nhw	They know
	Gŵyr hi	She knows		

The Conditional Tense

This can also be used to convey the Imperfect Tense.

	Singular		Plural
1 Gwyddwn i	I would know/ I knew	Gwydden ni	We would know/ We knew
2 Gwyddet ti	You would know/ You knew	Gwyddech chi	You would know/ You knew
3 Gwyddai fe/fo	He would know/ He knew	Gwydden nhw	They would know/ They knew
Gwyddai hi	She would know/ She knew		

Note—The short forms of the Future and Past Tenses are hardly ever used in speech.

DEFECTIVE VERBS

1 "DYLWN"

This verb is conjugated only in two tenses.

(a) "Dylwn i" etc. conveys the meaning "I ought/should" etc.

Affirmative *Singular*   *Plural*

	Singular		Plural
1 Dylwn i	I ought to/should	Dylen ni	We ought to/should
2 Dylet ti	You ought to/should	Dylech chi	You ought to/should
3 Dylai fe/fo	He ought to/should	Dylen nhw	They ought to/should
Dylai hi	She ought to/should		

Negative *Singular*   *Plural*

	Singular		Plural
1 Ddylwn i ddim	I ought not to/should not	Ddylen ni ddim	We ought not to/ should not
2 Ddylet ti ddim	You ought not to/ should not	Ddylech chi ddim	You ought not to/ should not
3 Ddylai fe/fo ddim	He ought not to/ should not	Ddylen nhw ddim	They ought not to/ should not
Ddylai hi ddim	She ought not to/ should not		

Interrogative *Singular*   *Plural*

	Singular		Plural
1 Ddylwn i?	Ought I to/Should I?	Ddylen ni?	Ought we to/Should we?
2 Ddylet ti?	Ought you to/Should you?	Ddylech chi?	Ought you to/Should you?
3 Ddylai fe/fo?	Ought he to/Should he?	Ddylen nhw?	Ought they to/Should they?
Ddylai hi?	Ought she to/Should she?		

Answer Forms

	Singular Yes/No	Plural Yes/No
1	Dylwn/Na ddylwn	Dylen/Na ddylen
2	Dylet/Na ddylet	Dylech/Na ddylech
3	Dylai/Na ddylai	Dylen/Na ddylen

e.g. Dylwn i wybod. — I ought to/should know.

Ddylai fe ddim mynd allan os oes annwyd arno fe. — He ought not to/should not go out if he's got a cold.

Ddylai'r plant wrando ar yr athro? — Ought the children to/Should the children listen to the teacher?

Dylen (dylai'r plant wrando ar yr athro). — Yes (the children ought to/should listen to the teacher).

Na ddylen (ddylai'r plant ddim gwrando ar yr athro). — No (the children ought not to/should not listen to the teacher).

Note that "dylen" (yes)/"na ddylen" (no) are used when the subject is plural.

(b) "Dylwn i" etc., followed by "fod" + "wedi" and verb-noun conveys the meaning "I ought to have/should have".

Affirmative

Dylwn i fod wedi, etc.   I ought to have/should have, etc.

Negative

Ddylwn i ddim bod wedi, etc.   I ought/should not have, etc.

(Note that "bod" is used after the negative form, "Ddylwn i ddim", etc.)

Interrogative

Ddylwn i fod wedi? etc.   Ought /Should I have? etc.

Answer Forms

	Singular Yes/No	Plural Yes/No
1	Dylwn/Na ddylwn	Dylen/Na ddylen
2	Dylet/Na ddylet	Dylech/Na ddylech
3	Dylai/Na ddylai	Dylen/Na ddylen

e.g. Dylwn i fod wedi mynd gyda hi. — I ought to/should have gone with her.

Ddylech chi ddim bod wedi dweud celwydd. — You ought not to/should not have lied.

Ddylai hi fod wedi ennill? — Ought she to/Should she have won?

Dylai (dylai hi fod wedi ennill). — Yes (she ought to/should have won).

Na ddylai (ddylai hi ddim bod wedi ennill). — No (she ought not to/shouldn't have won).

In literary Welsh the form "Dyl(a)swn i", etc., is used instead of "Dylwn i fod wedi", etc.

2 "MEDDWN"

The Present Tense

	Singular		Plural	
1	Meddaf i	I say	Meddwn ni	We say
2	Meddi di	You say	Meddwch chi	You say
3	Medd e/o	He says	Meddan nhw	They say
	Medd hi	She says		

The Imperfect Tense

	Singular		Plural	
1	Meddwn i	I said	Medden ni	We said
2	Meddet ti	You said	Meddech chi	You said
3	Meddai fe/fo	He said	Medden nhw	They said
	Meddai hi	She said		

"Meddwn i" and "Meddaf i" (the latter in its colloquial forms) are found in speech when quoting the actual words by speakers. These forms are mainly found in North Wales, whereas in South Wales the appropriate form of the verb "dweud" (to say) is used.

> e.g. "Rydw i'n mynd heddiw", meddai fe. ⎫ "I'm going today", he said.
> "Rydw i'n mynd heddiw", dywedodd e. ⎬

In addition to the above forms, an additional form "ebe" is only found in literary Welsh.

> e.g. "Maen nhw'n dod", ebe John.　　　"They're coming", says John.

THE IMPERATIVE MOOD (COMMAND FORMS OF THE VERB)

Second person singular and Second person plural

These commands are formed by adding the endings "-a" (second person singular) and "-wch" (second person plural) to the stem of the verb-noun. (See page 39 for information on stems of verb-nouns.)

(The second person singular is used when close friends talk to each other, parents speak to their children or people to their pets. In other instances the second person plural is used.)

> e.g. canu　　　can-a
> 　　　(to sing)　can-wch
> 　　　eistedd　　eistedd-a
> 　　　(to sit)　　eistedd-wch

The following are the command forms of irregular verbs.

bod	bydda
(to be)	byddwch
mynd	dos/cer
(to go)	ewch/cerwch
dod	tyrd/dere
(to come)	dowch/dewch
gwneud	gwna
(to do)	gwnewch
cael	cymera
(to have)	cymerwch

} see note on page 46

The direct object undergoes soft mutation after these command forms.

e.g. John, rhowch bunt.   John, give a pound.
     Gwnewch deisen i de, Mam.   Make a cake for tea, Mam.

The negative is formed by using "Paid" (second person singular) or "Peidiwch" (second person plural)—which mean "Don't" or "Stop"—before the verb-noun.

e.g. Paid rhedeg (sing.)   Don't run.

Peidiwch cerdded i'r dref. (pl.)   Don't walk to town.
Peidiwch aros. (pl.)   Don't wait.

In literary Welsh and in some dialects "Paid" and "Peidiwch" are followed by "â" (which causes aspirate mutation of p, t, c). This "â" becomes "ag" before a word beginning with a vowel.

e.g. Paid â chwerthin. (sing.)   Don't laugh.
     Peidiwch â thalu. (pl.)   Don't pay.
     Peidiwch ag edrych nawr. (pl.)   Don't look now.

This text-book, however, follows the practice of dialects where the "â/ag" is omitted.

Other Persons

The imperative is usually expressed by using "Gadewch i" (gadael i—to allow).

e.g. Gadewch i'r ferch ddod.   Let the girl come.

The preposition "i" has personal forms (see page 55).

1st person	(sing.)	Gadewch i fi ddarllen.	Let me read.
	(pl.)	Gadewch i ni fynd.	Let us go.
3rd person	(sing.)	Gadewch iddo fe yrru.	Let him drive.
		Gadewch iddi hi yrru.	Let her drive.
	(pl.)	Gadewch iddyn nhw fod.	Let them be.

Note that the verb-noun undergoes soft mutation after "Gadewch i fi/iddo fe", etc.

The Negative Forms

Paid gadael i fi redeg.   Don't let me run.

Peidiwch gadael i fi dalu.   Don't let me pay.

THE IMPERSONAL FORMS

The impersonal may be expressed:

1 By using the personal forms of the verb. It is often expressed in this way in speech.

  e.g. Maen nhw'n codi tai newydd yn y dref.   They are building new houses in the town.

      Mae pobl yn mwynhau drama dda.   People enjoy a good drama.

Although the personal forms of the verb are used in these sentences, they do not refer to any particular person/s.

2 By using the verb-noun "cael" + the personal pronouns ("fy, dy" etc.) + verb-noun.

  e.g. Mae'r parti'n cael ei gynnal heno.   The party is being held tonight.

      Roedd ffilm newydd yn cael ei dangos   A new film was being shown last night.
      neithiwr.

      Cafodd y ci ei ladd ar y ffordd.   The dog was killed on the road.

      Roeddwn i wedi cael fy siomi.   I had been disappointed.

      Byddan nhw'n cael eu gwahodd i'r parti. They will be invited to the party.

      Basai hi ddim yn cael ei dewis.   She would not be selected.

It is possible to convey all tenses of the verb with this construction by using the appropriate tense of "cael".

The preposition "gan/gyda" is used to denote the agent (or doer) of the deed.

  e.g. Mae e'n cael ei ddysgu gydag/gan   He is taught by a teacher from the
      athrawes o'r Rhondda.   Rhondda.

      Roedd yr arian wedi cael ei gasglu gyda/ The money had been collected by him.
      ganddo fe.

"Cael" can sometimes be left out after "wedi".

  e.g. Mae'r llyfr wedi cael ei sgrifennu'n dda. ⎫
      Mae'r llyfr wedi'i sgrifennu'n dda. ⎬ The book has been well-written.

      Roedd y gwaith wedi cael ei orffen mewn ⎫
      pryd. ⎬ The work had been finished in time.
      Roedd y gwaith wedi'i orffen mewn pryd. ⎭

The Traditional Impersonal Forms

The endings -ir (Present Tense), -id (Imperfect Tense), -wyd (Past Tense), -asid (Pluperfect Tense) are added to the stem of the verb-noun to form the Impersonal.

50

	Present Tense	Imperfect Tense	Past Tense	Pluperfect Tense
gweld (to see)	gwel-ir	gwel-id	gwel-wyd	gwel-asid
canu (to sing)	cen-ir	cen-id	can-wyd	can-asid

Note that where the vowel of the stem is **a**, it will change to **e** before the endings -ir, -id.

Generally speaking the Impersonal forms have died out in speech, except in the Past Tense.

e.g. Gwelwyd bod hynny'n wir.   It was seen that that was true.
Cadwyd y peth yn dawel.   The thing was kept quiet.

Note that the verb "geni" (to be born) has an alternative impersonal ending in the Past Tense—"gan-wyd" or "gan-ed" may be used.

e.g. Ganwyd ⎱ y bachgen yng Nghaerdydd.   The boy was born in Cardiff.
Ganed ⎰

PREPOSITIONS

Prepositions are followed by nouns or pronouns and can be divided into three categories.

1 Prepositions that are followed directly by nouns or independent pronouns.

e.g. gyda (with)	gyda Siân	with Siân
	gyda nhw	with them
efo (with-N.W.)	efo hi	with her
	efo nhw	with them
gyferbyn â (opposite)	gyferbyn â hi	opposite her
	gyferbyn â ni	opposite us
heblaw (besides)	heblaw John	besides John
	heblaw fi	besides me
i lawr (down)	i lawr y rhiw	down the hill
i fyny (up)	i fyny'r mynydd	up the mountain
tua(g) (about)	tua chwech	about six
rownd (around)	rownd y cornel	around the corner
mewn (in a)	mewn tŷ	in a house
ers (for = since)	ers mis	for (since) a month

2 Prepositions that are followed by nouns and are conjugated when a pronoun is added to them (i.e. the pronouns are incorporated in the endings).

Wrth (by)

Singular	Plural
1 wrtho i	wrthon ni
2 wrthot ti	wrthoch chi
3 wrtho fe/fo	wrthyn nhw
wrthi hi	

At (to, towards), Dan (under), Am ((amdan-) about), Ar ((arn-) on)

Singular	Plural
1 ata i	aton ni
2 atat ti	atoch chi
3 ato fe/fo	atyn nhw
ati hi	

Drwy/Trwy (through), Heb ((hebdd-) without), Rhag (rhagdd-)

Singular	Plural
1 drwyddo i	drwyddon ni
2 drwyddot ti	drwyddoch chi
3 drwyddo fe/fo	drwyddyn nhw
drwyddi hi	

Heb (without)

Singular	Plural
1 hebddo i	hebddon ni
2 hebbdot ti	hebddoch chi
3 hebddo fe/fo	hebddyn nhw
hebddi hi	

Rhwng (between)

Singular	Plural
1 rhyngo i	rhyngon ni
2 rhyngot ti	rhyngoch chi
3 rhyngddo fe/fo	rhyngddyn nhw
rhyngddi hi	

Yn (in)

Singular	Plural
1 yno i	ynon ni
2 ynot ti	ynoch chi
3 ynddo fe/fo	ynddyn nhw
ynddi hi	

Gan

Singular	Plural
1 gen i	gynnon ni
2 gen ti	gynnoch chi
3 ganddo fe/fo	ganddyn nhw
ganddi hi	

The meaning of "gan" depends upon the construction in which is it used. This will be dealt with in the appropriate sections of the notes on constructions.

"Gyda" instead of "Gan" is generally used in South Wales and is acceptable.

Singular	Plural
1 gyda fi	gyda ni
2 gyda ti	gyda chi
3 gyda fe/fo	gyda nhw
gyda hi	

e.g. Mae ci gyda fi.	I have a dog.

I (to, for)

Singular	Plural
1 i fi/mi	i ni
2 i ti	i chi
3 iddo fe/fo	iddyn nhw
iddi hi	

Similarly:

i mewn i (into)	y tu allan i (outside)
y tu draw i (the far side of)	y tu ôl i (behind)
y tu hwnt i (beyond)	y tu mewn i (inside)
heibio i (past)	

Dros/Tros (over, on behalf of, for)

Singular	Plural
1 drosto i	droston ni
2 drostot ti	drostoch chi
3 drosto fe/fo	drostyn nhw
drosti hi	

O (from)

Singular	Plural
1 ohono i	ohonon ni
2 ohonot ti	ohonoch chi
3 ohono fe/fo	ohonyn nhw
ohoni hi	

Similarly:

Mo (ddim o)

Singular	*Plural*
1 mono i	monon ni
2 monot ti	monoch chi
3 mono fe/fo	monyn nhw
moni hi	

3 Prepositions that conjugate by placing a pronoun between their two elements. e.g.

1. **ar draws (across)**

Singular	*Plural*
1 ar fy nhraws i	ar ein traws ni
2 ar dy draws di	ar eich traws chi
3 ar ei draws e/o	ar eu traws nhw
ar ei thraws hi	

(For mutations after "fy", "dy", etc., see page 28).

2 ar ôl (after)

Singular	*Plural*
1 ar fy ôl i	1 ar ein hôl ni
2 ar dy ôl di	2 ar eich ôl chi
3 ar ei ôl e/o	3 ar eu hôl nhw
ar ei hôl hi	

(The letter "h" appears before words beginning with a vowel after "ei" (f), "ein", "eu". This "h" is hardly discernible in speech. See page 28).

Similarly:

yn lle (instead)	yn fy lle i (instead of me)
ar gyfer (for)	ar fy nghyfer i (for me)
o gwmpas (around/about)	o fy nghwmpas i (around/about me)
o flaen (in front of)	o fy mlaen i (in front of me)
er mwyn (for the sake of)	er fy mwyn i (for my sake)
ar bwys (near—S.W.)	ar fy mhwys i (near me)
yn erbyn (against)	yn fy erbyn i (against me)
wrth ochr (by the side of)	wrth fy ochr i (by my side)
o amgylch (around)	o fy amgylch i (around me)
yn ymyl (near)	yn fy ymyl i (near me)

Sometimes the two elements that form the preposition have to be separated.

e.g. uwchben (uwch + pen) (above)	uwch fy mhen i (above me)
ymysg (yn + mysg) (among)	yn ein mysg ni (amongst us)

Note that the use of the preposition "gerllaw" is very restricted and when used is always followed by nouns.

e.g. gerllaw'r tŷ   nearby the house

When a pronoun is required the prepositions "yn ymyl" (yn fy ymyl i) or "wrth ochr" (wrth fy ochr i) are used instead of "gerllaw".

Verb-Nouns followed by Prepositions

Certain verb-nouns take prepositions after them. Here are some important examples.

RHAG

		WRTH		ODDI WRTH	
achub rhag	to save from	adrodd wrth	to relate to	lladrata oddi wrth	
rhybuddio rhag	to warn against	glynu wrth	to stick to		to steal from
amddiffyn rhag	to protect from	aros wrth	to stay/stop at		
atal rhag	to refrain from	dweud wrth	to tell		
cadw rhag	to keep from				
cilio rhag	to retreat from				
ffoi rhag	to flee from				
gwylio rhag	to beware of				

AT / I / AR

				AR	
anfon (at)	to send to (a person)	anfon i	to send to (a place)	galw ar	to call on
		llwyddo i	to succeed in	blino ar	to grow tired of
		gorfodi (rhywun) i	to compel (someone) to	dibynnu ar	to depend on
				edrych ar	to look at
				gweiddi ar	to shout at
				gwenu ar	to smile at
				gwrando ar	to listen to
				sylwi ar	to observe
				syllu ar	to gaze at
				tywynnu ar	to shine on
				ymosod ar	to attack

Â / AM / YN

		AM	
cwrdd â / cyfarfod â	to meet	breuddwydio am	to dream about
cymharu â	to compare with	cosbi am	to punish for
cymysgu â	to mix with	gofalu am	to take care of
siarad â	to talk to	meddwl am	to think about
ymadael â	to depart	pryderu am	to worry about
ymweld â	to visit		
cyffwrdd â	to touch	**YN**	
dod â	to bring	cydio yn	to join/grasp
mynd â	to take		
peidio â	to stop		

The following prepositions cause mutation:

Soft: am, ar, at, dan/tan, dros/tros, drwy/trwy, heb, i, o, wrth, gan, hyd.

Aspirate: gyda(g) tua(g). (These mutations are still found in some dialects and in literary Welsh but are not used in this text book.)

Nasal: yn.

Note that "ar hyd" (along) has personal endings:

ar hyd-ddo fe/fo	(along it)
ar hyd-ddi hi	(along it)
ar hyd-ddon nhw	(along them)

The verbs in the list below are followed immediately by another verb-noun without a preposition intervening.

addo (to promise)
anghofio (to forget)
arfer (to use, to be accustomed to)
blino (to become tired)
bwriadu (to intend)
bygwth (to threaten)
casáu (to hate)
ceisio (to seek, to try, to apply)
cofio (to remember)
cychwyn (to begin, to start)
dechrau (to begin)
dewis (to choose)
disgwyl (to expect)
dymuno (to wish)
dysgu (to learn, to teach)
eisiau/mofyn (to want, to need)
gallu (to be able to)
gobeithio (to hope)
gorffen (to finish)
gwrthod (to refuse)
haeddu (to deserve)
hoffi (to like)
meddwl (to think)
methu (to fail)
mwynhau (to enjoy)
mynnu (to insist)
ofni (to fear)
peidio (to cease, to stop)—but see note on page 51.
penderfynu (to decide, to resolve)
setlo (to settle)
synnu (to wonder, to surprise)

trefnu (to arrange)
trio (to try)
ymarfer (to practise)
ystyried (to consider)

e.g. Rydw i'n addo dod.   I promise to come.
    Roedd e wedi gwrthod darllen.   He had refused to read.

Note also that "gofyn i" is followed by a noun and verb-noun without a second preposition intervening. The verb-noun undergoes soft mutation.

e.g. Rydw i wedi gofyn i Alun ddod.   I have asked Alun to come.

ADVERBS

An adverb modifies a verb. It tells how, why, when, where or to what extent an action takes place.

As in English, most adverbs are formed from adjectives (e.g. quick—quickly). In Welsh the adverb is formed by placing "yn" in front of the adjective, which undergoes soft mutation except for words beginning with "ll" and "rh".

e.g. da (good) yn dda

   Gyrrodd hi'n dda.   She drove well.

   araf (slow) yn araf

   Mae'r hen ddyn yn cerdded yn araf.   The old man walks slowly.

   rhagorol (excellent) yn rhagorol

   Roedd hi'n gallu canu'r piano'n   She could play the piano excellently.
     rhagorol.

   llonydd (still) yn llonydd

   Roedd pawb yn eistedd yn llonydd.   Everyone was sitting still.

Similarly with the degrees of comparison:
e.g. gwell (better) yn well

   Mae hi'n edrych yn well heddiw.   She is looking better today.

   gwaeth (worse) yn waeth

   Rydw i'n gobeithio fydd e ddim yn   I hope he won't be feeling worse
     teimlo'n waeth yfory.   tomorrow.

But note that "yn" is always omitted when the equative degree of comparison is used adverbially and optionally omitted when the superlative degree is used adverbially.

e.g. cystal ⎫
    mor dda ⎬ (as good)

Mae e wedi gwneud cystal/mor dda â'i frawd.	He has done as well as his brother.

cynddrwg
mor ddrwg } (as bad)

Chwaraeon nhw ddim cynddrwg/mor ddrwg â'r tîm arall.	They didn't play as badly as the other team.

gorau   (best)

Gareth sy'n gallu canu orau yn y dosbarth.	It is Gareth who can sing best in the class.
P'un o'r bechgyn ddringodd ucha?	Which one of the boys climbed highest?

There are many adverbs in Welsh which occur naturally without having to be formed from adjectives.

e.g. heno (tonight)
eleni (this year)
ymlaen (on)

Mae e'n dod heno.	He's coming tonight.
Rydyn ni'n sefyll ein arholiadau eleni.	We're sitting our exams this year.
Dewch ymlaen.	Come on.

When a noun is used in an adverbial phrase it should undergo soft mutation but this is often broken in speech.

e.g. Gwelais i e ddydd Sadwrn diwetha.
Gwelais i e dydd Sadwrn diwetha. } I saw him last Saturday.

But when the adverb "pob" is used to form adverbial phrases soft mutation always occurs.

e.g. bob dydd   every day
bob amser   every time/always
bob blwyddyn   every year

Lled, Gweddol, Go (fairly/quite), Rhy (too) are followed by adjectives and cause soft mutation.

e.g. lled dda   yn lled dda
gweddol dda   yn weddol dda } (fairly/quite good/well)
go dda   yn o dda

rhy drwm   yn rhy drwm   (too heavy)
rhy lawn   yn rhy lawn   (too full)

Eithaf (fairly/quite) is followed by an adjective but it does not cause mutation.

e.g. eithaf mawr (fairly/quite big)   yn eithaf mawr.

Iawn (very), Dros ben (exceedingly) follow the adjective.

e.g. tal iawn (very tall)   yn dal iawn

byr dros ben (exceedingly short)   yn fyr dros ben

(Note that "iawn" can be used on its own to mean "proper, fine, correct, all right".

e.g. Roedd e'n edrych yn iawn beth bynnag.   He looked alright however).

Byth, Erioed (ever)/(never—when used with a negative verb).

"Byth" means "ever/never" in reference to future time.

e.g. Cymru am byth.   Wales for ever.
Dydw i byth eisiau mynd ar y cyfandir.   I never want to go on the continent.

"Erioed" means "ever/never" in reference to past time.

e.g. Fuoch chi'n aros ym Mharis erioed?   Have you ever stayed in Paris?
Dydw i ddim wedi bod ar y cyfandir   I have never been on the continent.
erioed.

Bron (almost), Braidd (rather). When followed by an adjective, "yn" is placed before the adjective.

e.g. Roedd y neuadd yn edrych bron yn   The hall looked almost full.
llawn.

Mae hi'n teimlo braidd yn oer.   She feels rather cold.

Adre (homewards), gartre (at home).

Note the difference between "adre" (homewards) and "gartre" (at home).

e.g. *Adre:*   Ble rydych chi'n mynd? Adre. Where are you going? Home(wards).

Gartre: Bydda i'n aros gartre heno.   I shall be staying (at) home tonight.

Demonstrative Adverbs

"**Dyma**" is used to express the meaning "here is/are" when the noun/pronoun which follows is in close proximity to the speaker.

e.g. Dyma John.   Here is John.
Dyma'r llyfr.   Here is the book.
Dyma'r bechgyn.   Here are the boys.
Dyma nhw.   Here they are.

"**Dyna**" is generally used to express surprise, astonishment and agreement or a vague "that" where there is no demonstrative element involved.

e.g. Dyna ryfedd.   That's strange.

Dyna fe.   That's it. (i.e. You've got it.)

Dyna chi.   There you are (i.e. That's it).

Dyna dda.   There's good. That's good. How good.

Dyna ddiwedd y stori.   That's the end of the story.

But "**Dyna**" can be used to express the meaning "there is/are" when the noun/pronoun which follows is not in close proximity to the speaker.

e.g. Dyna Siân.   There is Siân.

Dyna hi.   There she is.

Dyna'r plant.   There are the children.

"**Dacw**" however is used generally as a demonstrative adverb when the noun/pronoun is not in close proximity.

e.g. Dacw Siân.   There is Siân.

"**Yma**", "**Yna**" ("**Yno**" in N.W.) are used to convey the meanings "here", "there" when the precise location is not indicated. (In speech these tend to become "ma", "na".)

e.g. Dewch yma.   Come here.

Mae'r bechgyn yna.   The boys are there.

"**Acw**" in North Wales is also used to convey the meaning "there" but this is not found in South Wales.

e.g. Mae'r merched acw.   The girls are there (=over there).

The phrases "Dewch acw", "Dewch draw" are often used to express the meaning "come over" (i.e. to our house).

"**Fan yma**", "**Fan yna**" are used when the precise location is indicated.

e.g. Eisteddwch fan yma.   Sit here (in this spot).

Mae'r llyfr fan yna (ar y bwrdd).   The book is there (on the table).

CONJUNCTIONS

The following conjunctions can join words, clauses or sentences.

1 A/ag (and)

"A" is used in front of consonants (including "h").

e.g. brawd a chwaer   brother and sister

tad a mam   father and mother

pupur a halen   pepper and salt

In literary Welsh and in some dialects "a" causes aspirate mutation of c, p, t.

e.g. bara a chaws   bread and cheese
      pen a phensil   pen and pencil
      mam a thad   mother and father

However, in other dialects, this rule no longer operates and this text book follows that practice.

e.g. bara a caws, pen a pensil, mam a tad.

"Ag" is used in front of vowels.

e.g. Cerddodd e i mewn i'r stafell ag agorodd   He walked into the room and opened
      y ffenestr.   the window.

2 Na/nag (nor)

Does dim diod na bwyd yn y tŷ.   There's no drink nor food in the house.

Dydw i ddim eisiau oren nag afal.   I don't want an apple nor an orange.

The same rules of mutation apply to "na" and "a". (See above.)

3 Ond (but)

e.g. Rydw i'n dod ond mae e'n aros yn y tŷ.   I'm coming but he's staying in the
                                              house.

Note also the special use of "ond" after a negative verb to express the meaning "only".

e.g. Ddywedais i ddim ond y gwir.   I said nothing but the truth.
                                            (I only said the truth.)

4 Neu (or)

e.g. gŵr neu wraig   husband or wife
      ennill neu golli   win or lose
      du neu goch   black or red

Note that "neu" causes soft mutation when it is followed by nouns, verb-nouns or adjectives.

When it is followed by an inflected form of the verb, no mutation occurs.
e.g. Ewch allan neu byddwch yn dawel.   Go out or be quiet.

Other conjunctions used to link clauses are dealt with in the sections on Subordinate Clauses.

THE GENITIVE CASE

When a noun is dependent upon the noun which precedes it in order to show ownership, that noun is said to be in the genitive cause.

e.g. Mam Huw.   Huw's mother.

This is expressed in English by "'s", "s'" and "of".

e.g. The man's hand.
     Gareth's book.
     The boys' school.
     The bottom of the hill.
     The capital of Wales.

The Welsh construction is arrived at as follows:

In the phrase "the capital of Wales" delete the "the" at the beginning and the "of" in the middle of the phrase:

i.e. (the) capital   (of) Wales
         capital   Wales
         prifddinas   Cymru

Similarly:

     (the) bottom   (of) the hill
          bottom   the hill
          gwaelod   y bryn

In the phrase "the man's hand", rewrite this in the long form.

i.e. the hand of the man

Proceeding as above we have—

     (the) hand   (of) the man
          llaw   y dyn

Similarly:

     Gareth's book

i.e. (the) book   (of) Gareth
         llyfr   Gareth

     the   boys' school
     (the) school   (of) the boys
          ysgol   y bechgyn

This method can also be applied when there are two nouns in the genitive case in the same phrase.

e.g. the price of the boy's book

i.e. (the) price (of the) book (of) the boy
         pris   llyfr   y bachgen

Note that the only position where the definite article can occur is before the final noun.

When the genitive expresses quantity, the phrase is translated into Welsh as it stands in English (i.e. by using "o"—of).

e.g. a pint of milk   peint o laeth
    a sack of potatoes   sachaid o datws
    a cup of tea   cwpanaid o de

BOD + GAN/GYDA = TO HAVE, TO POSSESS

The verb "Bod" (to be) is used with the appropriate forms of the prepositions "gan/gyda" to express possession in Welsh.

e.g. Mae car gan Gwyn.
Mae car gyda Gwyn.   } Gwyn has a car.

Mae ci ganddyn nhw.
Mae ci gyda nhw.   } They have a dog.

The preposition "gan" is used in literary Welsh and in many dialects. For the conjugated forms of "gan" see page 55. The preposition "gyda" is generally used in S. Wales and this text book follows that practice.

The Present Tense of the verb "Bod" followed by a noun/pronoun and "gyda" expresses the meaning "I have/I've got . . . etc.", in English. Note that the verb is always in the third person singular.

Definite Noun/Pronoun

Mae'r llyfr gyda hi.   She's got the book.
Ydy'r llyfr gyda hi?   Has she got the book?
Dydy'r llyfr ddim gyda hi.   She hasn't got the book.

Indefinite Noun

Mae cath gyda nhw.   They've got a cat.
Oes cath gyda nhw?   Have they got a cat?
Does dim cath gyda nhw.   They haven't got a cat.

"Mae" changes to "oes" in the interrogative and in the negative when the subject is indefinite and to "ydy" when the subject is definite.

The Imperfect Tense of the verb "Bod" followed by a noun/pronoun and "gyda" expresses the meaning "I had/I had got . . . etc.", in English.

Definite Noun/Pronoun

Roedd e gyda fe.	He had it.
Oedd e gyda fe?	Did he have it?
Doedd e ddim gyda fe.	He didn't have it.

Indefinite Noun

Roedd teledu gyda ni.	We had a television.
Oedd teledu gyda ni?	Did we have a television?
Doedd dim teledu gyda ni.	We didn't have a television.

The Future Tense of the verb "Bod" followed by a noun/pronoun and "gyda" expresses the meaning "I will have . . ." etc. in English.

Definite Noun/Pronoun

Bydd yr arian gyda John yfory.	John will have the money tomorrow.
Fydd yr arian gyda John yfory?	Will John have the money tomorrow?
Fydd yr arian ddim gyda John yfory.	John will not have the money tomorrow.

Indefinite Noun

Bydd amser gyda chi.	You will have time.
Fydd amser gyda chi?	Will you have time?
Fydd dim amser gyda chi.	You will not have time.

The Conditional Tense of the verb "Bod" followed by a noun/pronoun and "gyda" expresses the meaning "I would have . . ." etc. in English.

Definite Noun/Pronoun

Basai fe gyda fe.	He would have it.
Fasai fe gyda fe?	Would he have it?
Fasai fe ddim gyda fe.	He wouldn't have it.

Indefinite Noun

Basai arian gyda nhw.	They would have money.
Fasai arian gyda nhw?	Would they have money?
Fasai dim arian gyda nhw.	They wouldn't have any money.

When the noun/pronoun precedes the verb, the appropriate form of the verb used in the Present Tense is "sy".

e.g. Car sy gyda fe.	He's got a **car.**

In the negative form "dim" precedes the noun/pronoun.

e.g. Dim car sy gyda fe.	He hasn't got a **car.**

Note

There are three uses of the English "has/have" and it is important to be familiar with these uses.

1 Has/have = to possess

  e.g. Mae gwallt du gyda fi.   I have black hair.
       Mae tei glas gyda fe.   He has a blue tie.

2 Has/have = to receive/to get

  This is expressed by the verb "cael".

  e.g. Rydw i'n cael wy i frecwast bob dydd.   I have an egg for breakfast every day.

       Mae e'n cael cwpanaid o goffi cyn mynd   He has a cup of coffee before going to
        i'r gwely.   bed.

3 Has/have = the Perfect Tense of the verb.

  e.g. Rydw i wedi dod.   I have come.
       Mae e wedi cyrraedd.   He has arrived.

IDIOMATIC CONSTRUCTIONS BASED ON THE PREPOSITIONS AR, GAN/ GYDA AND I

1 AR

Note the use of the preposition "ar" with the third person singular of the verb "Bod" in the following idioms:

Mae syched arna i.	I am thirsty.
Mae hiraeth arna i.	I long for.
Mae ofn arna i.	I am afraid.
Mae cywilydd arna i.	I am ashamed.
Mae chwant arna i.	I have a desire.

Further examples

Oes syched arnoch chi?	Are you thirsty?
Roedd hiraeth ar y ferch am ei chartref.	The girl longed for her home.
Doedd dim ofn arno fe o gwbl.	He wasn't at all frightened.
Bydd chwant bwyd arnyn nhw ar ôl bod allan yn chwarae.	They'll have a desire for/They'll long for food after being out playing.

This construction is also used when referring to illness.

  e.g. Mae annwyd arna i.   I have a cold.
       Roedd y ffliw arno fe.   He had the "flu".
       Mae'r frech goch arni hi.   She's got measles.
       Roedd brech yr ieir arnoch chi.   You had chicken pox.
       Ydy'r ddannoedd arnat ti?   Have you got toothache?
       Oes peswch arnyn nhw?   Have they got a cough?
       Does dim poen arna i.   I haven't got a pain.

But when a particular part of the body is mentioned the construction using "gyda"/ "gan" is used. See page 69(2).

Note that "Mae arna i . . ." etc., is used to express "I owe . . ." This is followed by soft mutation.

e.g. Mae arna i bunt.   I owe a pound.

Similarly:

Mae arna i bum ceiniog i Gareth.   I owe Gareth five pence.

Note the use of the preposition "i" in front of the indirect object Gareth.

"Mae eisiau . . . arna i" etc., is used to express "I need" etc.

e.g. Mae eisiau esgidiau newydd arna i. I need new shoes.

Further examples

Mae eisiau asprin arnat ti os oes pen tost gyda ti. | You need an aspirin if you've got a headache.
Bydd eisiau teiars newydd arnoch chi cyn bo hir. | You will need new tyres before long.
Welais i ddim ci mor denau â fe erioed. Roedd eisiau bwyd arno fe'n druenus. | I have never seen such a thin dog as he. He needed food badly.

However "I want . . ." etc., is conveyed by "Rydw i eisiau . . ."etc.

e.g. Rydw i eisiau mynd.   I want to go.
     Mae e eisiau pêl-droed.   He wants a football.
     Rydyn ni eisiau byw yn y wlad.   We want to live in the country.

Further Examples

Oedd e eisiau mynd i Gaerdydd?   Did he want to go to Cardiff?
Fyddan nhw ddim eisiau te, gobeithio.   They won't want tea, I hope.
Basai hi eisiau dod, rydw i'n siŵr.   She would want to come, I'm sure.

Note that "yn" is not used before "eisiau".

An alternative form used to convey the meaning "Rydw i eisiau" ("I want") is "Rydw i'n moyn/mofyn". This is chiefly used in South Wales.

e.g. Rydyn ni'n moyn/mofyn arian.   We want some money.
     Oeddech chi'n moyn/mofyn gweld   Did you want to see Rhodri?
     Rhodri?
     Fydda i ddim yn moyn/mofyn mynd   I won't want to go there again.
     yna eto.

2 GAN/GYDA

The preposition "gan/gyda" is used with the third person singular of the verb "Bod" in the following idioms:

Mae (hi)'n dda gyda fi.	I'm pleased/glad.
Mae (hi)'n ddrwg gyda fi.	I'm sorry.
Mae (hi)'n flin gyda fi.	I'm sorry.
Mae (hi)'n gas gyda fi.	I hate.
Mae (hi)'n well gyda fi.	I prefer.

Further examples

Mae (hi)'n dda gyda ni gwrdd â chi.	We are pleased to meet you.
Roedd hi'n ddrwg gyda hi glywed.	She was sorry to hear.
Basai (hi)'n well gyda fi fynd i'r cyngerdd.	I would prefer to go to the concert.
Mae (hi)'n gas gyda fe waith cartref.	He hates homework.

Note that soft mutation occurs after these idioms.

After "mae" and "basai" the "hi" is hardly audible and need not be written. It must, however, be included in the interrogative and negative forms of these tenses and with all forms of the other tenses.

The construction using "gan/gyda" is also used when a particular part of the body is mentioned when referring to illness.

e.g. Mae pen tost gyda fi.	I've got a headache.
Mae gwddw tost gyda Siân.	Siân has got a sore throat.
Roedd stumog dost gyda fe ddoe.	He had a bad stomach yesterday.
Oes clustiau tost gyda chi?	Have you got earache?
Oedd cefn tost gyda hi?	Did she have a backache?

3 I

The preposition "i" is used with the third person singular of the verb "Bod" in certain idioms:

e.g. Mae rhaid i fi.	I must

Further examples

Mae rhaid i fi fynd.	I must go.

(Note that "Mae" is sometimes omitted.)

e.g. Rhaid i fi fynd.	I must go.
Does dim rhaid iddo fe godi'n gynnar heddiw.	He doesn't have to get up early today.
Fydd rhaid i chi siarad yn y cyfarfod, tybed?	Will you have to speak in the meeting, I wonder?
Doedd dim rhaid iddyn nhw fynd adre'n gynnar.	They didn't have to go home early.

Note that the verb-noun undergoes soft mutation after these idioms.

Similarly:

Mae'n well i fi . . .	It is better for me . . .
Mae'n bryd i fi . . .	It is time for me . . .
Mae'n hen bryd i fi . . .	It is high time for me . . .

Further examples

Mae'n well i fi fod yn dawel.	It is better for me to be quiet.
Dydy hi ddim yn bryd i fi fynd i'r gwely eto.	It isn't time for me to go to bed yet.
Roedd hi'n hen bryd iddo fe godi.	It was high time for him to get up.
Mae'n well i fi beidio bwyta gormod.	It is better for me not to eat too much.

Note that "Mae rhaid i fi" etc., can also be followed by the mutated form of "peidio" (beidio) + verb-noun to convey the meaning "I must not" etc.

e.g. Mae rhaid i fi beidio mynd.	I must not go.
Mae rhaid i fi beidio gweiddi.	I must not shout.

THE SENTENCE

A. SIMPLE SENTENCES

(1) Sentences containing the inflected form of the verb.

The normal order of words in a simple sentence in Welsh is:

Verb + Subject + Rest of the sentence.

e.g. Gwelodd + Gareth + y ferch.	Gareth saw the girl.

Such sentences may be extended by inserting

(*a*) An adverb (or adverbial phrase) to modify the verb.

e.g. Gwelodd Gareth y ferch ddoe.	Gareth saw the girl yesterday.
Aeth y bachgen i'r llyfrgell cyn te.	The boy went to the library before tea.

(*b*) An adjective (or adjectival phrase) to describe the subject or/and object.

e.g. Prynodd Siân got newydd.	Siân bought a new coat.
Prynodd Siân esgidiau (gyda) sodlau uchel.	Siân bought high-heel shoes.

(2) Sentences containing the verb "Bod" (to be).

When the verb comes first in the affirmative sentences without any emphasis, the form used in the Present Tense must be "mae". It will be followed by the subject and one of the following.

(*a*) Adverb/Adverbial phrase.

e.g. Mae e yn y tŷ.	He's in the house.

The interrogative/negative form of "Mae" is "Ydy . . .?"/"Dydy . . . ddim" when the subject is definite and "Oes . . .?"/"Does dim . . ." when the subject is indefinite.

e.g. Ydy e yn yr ysgol heddiw?   Is he in school today?
Dydy Gareth ddim yn y parc.   Gareth isn't in the park.
Oes siwgr yn y cwpwrdd?   Is there any sugar in the cupboard?

Further examples using the other tenses of the verb "Bod".

Fyddwch chi wrth yr arhosfan?   Will you be at the bus stop?
Buodd y plant ym Mhorthcawl.   The children went to Porthcawl.
Pe basai fe yma . . .   If he were here . . .
Oedd e yn yr ysgol?   Was he in the school?
Doedden nhw ddim yn y gêm.   They weren't in the game.
Bydda i yna.   I shall be there.
Fuest ti yn y cyngerdd?   Did you go to the concert?
Roedd y plant ar y cae.   The children were on the field.

(b) "yn"/"wedi" + verb-noun.

e.g. Mae Gareth yn rhedeg.   Gareth is running.

Similarly:

Oes merched yn dod hefyd?   Are there girls coming too?
Ydy'r plant yn gwybod?   Do the children know?
Dydy e ddim yn cerdded.   He is not walking.
Fyddan nhw'n aros?   Will they be waiting?
Bues i'n gweithio yn Aberystwyth am   I worked in Aberystwyth for years.
  flynyddoedd.
Pe basech chi'n darllen . . .   If you were to read . . .
Ydyn nhw wedi bod yn siopa?   Have they been shopping?
Doeddet ti ddim wedi bod yn cysgu.   You hadn't been sleeping.
Bydd e'n chwarae.   He will be playing.
Fuodd Mr. Rhys yn dysgu Cymraeg yn   Did Mr. Rhys teach Welsh in school
  yr ysgol?

(c) "yn" + indefinite noun.

e.g. Mae hi'n ferch glyfar.   She's a clever girl.

Similarly:

Ydy'r dyn yn arlunydd da?   Is the man a good artist?
Dydy e ddim yn fachgen drwg.   He isn't a naughty boy.
Maen nhw'n blant swnllyd.   They're noisy children.
Fydd e'n athro da?   Will he be a good teacher?
Fuest ti'n siopwr am flwyddyn?   Were you a shopkeeper for a year?
Pe basai fe'n chwraewr rygbi...   If he were a rygby player...
Oedd y dyn yn nyrs?   Was the man a nurse?
Doeddwn i ddim yn bennaeth.   I wasn't a headteacher.
Bydd y bachgen yn chwaraewr da.   The boy will be a good player.
Fuon nhw'n forwyr yn ystod y rhyfel?   Were they sailors during the war?
Oedd hi'n blismon?   Was she a policeman?

(*d*) "yn" + adjective.

e.g. Mae Gareth yn drist.   Gareth is sad.

Similarly:

Ydy e'n fodlon?	Is he willing?
Dydy Aled ddim yn dal.	Aled isn't tall.
Doedd y ferch ddim yn fach.	The girl wasn't small.
Fyddi di'n hapus yna?	Will you be happy there?
Buon ni'n swnllyd yn ystod y nos.	We were noisy during the night.
Pe baswn i ddim mor hen . . .	If I weren't so old . . .
Ydych chi'n denau?	Are you thin?
Doeddwn i ddim yn dew.	I wasn't fat.
Byddan nhw'n rhy swil.	They will be too shy.
Buoch chi'n dwp.	You were stupid.
Roeddwn i'n ifanc.	I was young.

When the affirmative sentence consists of a definite subject, the verb "is/are" and a definite noun/pronoun complement, the verb used in the Present Tense is "ydy" and the word order is the same as in English.

i.e. Subject + Verb + Complement.

The verb is always in the third person singular whether the subject be a singular or plural noun or any personal pronoun.

e.g. Mr. Jones ydy'r prifathro newydd.   Mr. Jones is the new headmaster.

Note that the negative is formed by placing "dim" at the beginning of the sentence.

e.g. Dim yr athro Ffrangeg ydy'r athro   The French teacher isn't the best
      gorau.   teacher.

(In literary Welsh this negative form is expressed by: "Nid + affirmative construction.
e.g. Nid yr athro Ffrangeg ydy'r athro gorau).

The interrogative is conveyed simply by changing the intonation of the voice.

e.g. Nhw ydy'r plant tawel?   Are they the quiet children?

(In literary Welsh the interrogative is expressed by the interrogative particle "Ai?".
e.g. Ai nhw ydy'r plant tawel?

However this is no longer heard in speech).

B EMPHATIC SENTENCES

(1) Sentences containing the inflected form of the verb.

When emphasis is needed in a particular part of the sentence, that part is placed first and joined to the rest of the sentence by means of the relative pronoun "a" with soft mutation, or by the particle "y/yr".

(*a*) Subject emphasised.

Fy nhad (a) brynodd y teledu yna.   My *father* bought that television.

Fy chwaer (a) daliff am y llyfr.	*My sister* will pay for the book.
Y plant yma (a) dorrodd y ffenestr.	*These children* broke the window.

Note that the verb is always in the third person singular after the relative pronoun "a" even when the subject is a plural noun or any one of the personal pronouns.

e.g. Y bechgyn (a) dorrodd y ffenestr.	*The boys* broke the window.
Ni (a) welodd y bachgen.	*We* saw the boy.
Nhw (a) yfodd y pop.	*They* drank the pop.

(*b*) Object emphasised.

Y teledu yna (a) brynodd fy nhad.	My father bought *that television.*
Y comic yna (a) ddarlleniff fy chwaer.	My sister will read *that comic.*

Note that the relative pronoun "a" is often omitted in speech, although the mutation it causes remains.

(*c*) Any other part of the sentence emphasised.

Ddoe (y) prynodd fy nhad y teledu.	My father bought the television *yesterday.*

The particle "y/yr" is usually omitted in speech.

(Note that if the verb needs to be emphasised the auxiliary verb "gwneud" must be used.

e.g. Prynodd fy nhad y teledu.	My father bought the television.
Prynu 'r teledu (a) wnaeth fy nhad.	My father *bought* the television.

The Negative Form

The most common form in speech is:

Dim + affirmative construction.

e.g. Dim fy nhad (a) brynodd y teledu yma.	My *father* didn't buy this television.
Dim y teledu yma (a) brynodd fy nhad .	My father didn't buy *this television.*
Dim ddoe (y) prynodd fy nhad y teledu yna.	My father didn't buy that television *yesterday.*
Dim prynu'r teledu (a) wnaeth fy nhad .	My father didn't *buy* the television.

In literary Welsh the negative form is expressed by:

"Nid" + affirmative construction.

e.g. Nid fy nhad (a) brynodd y teledu yma.	My *father* didn't buy that television.

The Interrogative Form

This is expressed in speech by the affirmative form, with interrogative intonation.

e.g. Fy nhad (a) brynodd y teledu yna? Did *my father* buy this television?

Y teledu yna (a) brynodd fy nhad? Did my father buy *that television*?

Ddoe (y) prynodd fy nhad y teledu yna? Did my father buy that television *yesterday*?

The interrogative form in literary Welsh is introduced by the interrogative particle "Ai?"

e.g. Ai fy nhad (a) brynodd y teledu yma? Did *my father* buy this television?

This is no longer heard in speech.

(2) Sentences containing the verb "Bod" (to be)

1 When any of the following elements, which in the simple sentence come after "Mae" is placed first in the sentence for emphasis, "Mae" is retained, i.e.

(*a*) When an adverb/adverbial phrase occurs at the beginning of the sentence.

e.g. Yn y tŷ mae Huw. Huw is *in the house*.

Dim yn yr ysgol mae e wedi bod. He hasn't been *in school*.

Similarly:

Llynedd buoch chi yn Ffrainc? Did you go to France *last year*?
Yna roedd e'n gweithio. He was working *there*.
Yng Nghaerdydd basen nhw'n hoffi byw? Would they like to live *in Cardiff*?
Dim yn Abertawe bydd y gêm. The game won't be *in Swansea*.

(*b*) When a verb-noun occurs at the beginning of the sentence. (Note that "yn" is omitted but "wedi" is retained.)

e.g. Darllen mae Siân. Siân is *reading*.
Cysgu mae hi. She is *sleeping*.

Similarly:

Dim golchi bydd hi heno, gobeithio. She won't be *washing* tonight, I hope.
Wedi adrodd roedd e? Had he *recited*?
Chwarae rygbi basen nhw'n hoffi ar ôl te? Would they like *to play rugby* after tea?

(*c*) When an indefinite noun occurs at the beginning of a sentence.

e.g. Tŷ mae e'n beintio.   He is painting a *house*.
     Fflat maen nhw'n brynu?   Are they buying a *flat*?

Similarly:

Dim llyfr roedd e eisiau.	He didn't want a *book*.
Llythyr roedd e'n sgrifennu.	He was writing a *letter*.
Cot bydd e'n gael?	Will he be having a *coat*?
Pêl-droed basai fe'n hoffi.	He would like a *football*.

Note that the verb-noun undergoes soft mutation.

2 When the complement—noun or adjective—is placed first for emphasis, "ydy" is the form of the third person singular in the Present Tense.

e.g. Ficer ydy Mr. Jones.   Mr. Jones is a vicar.
     Dim du ydy lliw ei gar ei.   The colour of his car isn't *black*.

Similarly:

Glöwr oedd ei dad e.	His father was a *collier*.
Glas oedd y ffrog?	Was the frock *blue*?
Athrawes fydd hi rhyw ddiwrnod, gobeithio.	She will be a *teacher* some day, I hope.
Nhw fasai'r plant gorau.	*They* would be the best children.
Nyrs fuodd e am flynyddoedd.	He was a *nurse* for years.

Note that the "r" of "rydw i" etc., "roeddwn i" etc., is omitted in this emphatic sentence. Note also that "bydda i" etc., "bues i" etc., and "baswn i" etc., undergo soft mutation in this construction.

e.g. Hir oedden nhw.   They were *long*.
     Nyrs ydw i.   I am a *nurse*.
     Twpsyn fasech chi.   You would be a *fool*.
     Araf fyddwn ni.   We will be *slow*.

3 When the subject—noun or pronoun—is placed first for emphasis, "sy" is the form of the third person singular in the Present Tense. "Sy" in turn will be followed by one of these four elements.

i.e. (*a*) Adverb/Adverbial phrase.

e.g. Gareth sy yma.   *Gareth* is here.
     Fe sy yn y ffilm.   *He's* in the film.

Similarly:

Y newyddion fydd ar y teledu.	*The news* will be on the television.
Nhw oedd yn y tîm.	*They* were in the team.

(b) "yn"/"wedi" + verb-noun.

e.g. John sy'n rhedeg.   *John* is running.
     Fe sy wedi ennill.   *He* has won.

Similarly:

    Y ferch oedd yn darllen.   *The girl* was reading.
    Hi fydd yn mynd?   Will *she* be going?
    Dim Mair fasai wedi cael y swydd.   *Mair* would not have had the post.

(c) "yn" + indefinite noun.

e.g. Gareth sy'n fachgen da.   *Gareth* is a good boy.
     Nhw sy'n blant talentog.   *They* are talented children.

Similarly:

    Siân oedd yn ferch ddrwg ddoe.   *Siân* was a naughty girl yesterday.
    Fe fydd yn gapten y flwyddyn nesa.   *He* will be captain next year.

(d) "yn" + adjective.

e.g. Llaeth sy'n dda i chi.   *Milk* is good for you.

Similarly:

    Y cawl oedd yn dda.   The *broth* was good.
    Dim nhw oedd yn swnllyd.   *They* weren't noisy.
    Y bechgyn fydd yn ddrwg?   Will the *boys* be naughty?

Note that in other tenses the mutation form of the verb will be used, i.e. "fydd", "fuodd" and "fasai".

Note:

The distinction between "mae" on the one hand and "sy" and "ydy" on the other, illuminates another point of difference.

(a) In those circumstances where "mae" is used, the appropriate form of the verb in other persons and tenses is as follows:

Present Tense	Imperfect Tense	Past Tense	Future Tense	Conditional Tense
"Rydw i" etc.	"Roeddwn i" etc.	"Bues i" etc.	"Bydda i" etc.	"Baswn i" etc.

Note that "maen nhw" is used in the third person plural in the Present Tense. Note also the use of the "R" in the Present and Imperfect Tenses.

There is no soft mutation in the affirmative form of the Past, Future and Conditional Tenses.

(b) Where "sy" is used, the appropriate form in the other tenses is as follows:

Imperfect Tense	Past Tense	Future Tense	Conditional Tense
Oedd . . .	Fuodd . . .	Fydd . . .	Fasai . . .

Note the soft mutation in these tenses.

(c) Where "ydy" is used following the subject, the form in the other tenses is as follows:

Imperfect Tense	Past Tense	Future Tense	Conditional Tense
Oedd . . .	Fuodd . .	Fydd . . .	Fasai . . .

(d) Where "ydy" is used following the noun or adjective complement, the appropriate form in the other persons and tenses is as follows:

Present Tense	Imperfect Tense	Past Tense	Future Tense	Conditional Tense
Ydw i, etc.	Oeddwn i, etc.	Fues i, etc.	Fydda i, etc.	Faswn i, etc.

Note that soft mutation occurs in these tenses.

See also the section dealing with the interrogatives for the correct uses of these verbal forms after various interrogatives.

RELATIVE CLAUSES

1 INFLECTED VERBS

The relative pronoun as the subject or object of the inflected verb is "a".

e.g. Roedd y ffilm (a) welais i yn wael.   The film that I saw was poor.

Dyma'r plant (a) dorrodd y ffenestr.   Here are the children who broke the window.

Note that when "a" is the subject of the relative clause it is always followed by a verb in the third person singular.

This relative pronoun is no longer used in speech but the soft mutation it causes remains.

e.g. Mae'r esgidiau brynais i'n rhy fach.   The shoes I bought are too small.

The negative form of the relative "a" is "na" before verbs beginning with consonants and "nad" before verbs beginning with vowels (with "ddim" optional).

"Na" causes:

(*a*) Aspirate mutation when the verb begins with c, p, t.

(*b*) Soft mutation when the verb begins with g, b, d, ll, m, rh.

e.g. Dyma'r ferch na thalodd (ddim) am ei bwyd.

Here is the girl who didn't pay for her food.

Dyma'r bachgen na ofynnodd (ddim) am ei fwyd.

Here's the boy who didn't ask for his his food.

Adroddodd e stori nad anghofia i (ddim) am flynyddoedd.

He told a story which I shall not forget for years.

However, the relative pronoun "na" is often omitted in speech although the mutations it causes remain. When "na" is omitted "ddim" must be used.

e.g. Mae'r fenyw chafodd ddim gwahoddiad i'r briodas wedi digio.

The woman who didn't have an invitation to the wedding has taken offence.

Note that the relative pronoun when it is the subject of the verb is always followed by a verb in the third person singular even when the verb refers back to a plural noun.

e.g. Mae'r plant (nad) aeth ddim ar drip yr ysgol wedi cael mynd adre'n gynnar.

The children who didn't go on the school trip have been allowed to go home early.

2 THE VERB "BOD" (TO BE)

(*a*) "Sy" (who is, who are, which is, which are) is the relative form of the third person singular Present Tense which follows the subject.

e.g. Dylai'r ddrama sy ar y teledu heno fod yn dda.

The play which is on the television tonight should be good.

The negative form which is widely used in speech is "sy ddim".

e.g. Dyma'r tîm sy ddim wedi ennill gêm eleni.

Here's the team which hasn't won a game this year.

The literary form of the relative pronoun "sy" is "nad ydy" (who/which is/has not), with the "ddim" optional.

e.g. Dyma'r tîm nad ydy e (ddim) wedi ennill gêm eleni.

Here's the team which hasn't won a game this year.

(*b*) When the relative pronoun is in the object case in relation to the verb in the subordinate clause in English, "sy" cannot be used. The antecedent is followed by the appropriate form of the verb "Bod".

In the Present and Imperfect Tense the "r" is retained, e.g. "rydw i" etc., "roeddwn i" etc. In the case of the other tenses of "Bod", no mutation occurs e.g. "bydda i" etc., "bues i" etc., "baswn i" etc. The verb will be followed by its subject + "yn/ wedi" + verb-noun which undergoes soft mutation.

e.g. Ble mae'r llyfrau rydych chi wedi ddarllen?

Where are the books which you have read?

(For an explanation of this soft mutation, see page 103(4).

Rydw i'n adnabod y ferch roedd e'n hoffi. I know the girl which he used to like.

Ydych chi wedi clywed y gân bydda i'n ganu yfory?

Have you heard the song which I shall be singing tomorrow?

3 In the genitive case the relative form used is "y" ("yr" before vowels). This is followed by the verb and the pronoun "ei" (m.), "ei" (f.) and "eu" (pl.) in agreement with the antecedent.

The "y/yr" can be omitted.

e.g. Dyma'r ferch (y) cafodd ei thad ei ladd. Here's the girl whose father was killed.

The antecedent is "ferch" therefore "ei" before "thad" is feminine.

Similarly:

Dyma'r bachgen (y) cafodd ei dad ei ladd. Here's the boy whose father was killed.

The antecedent is "bachgen" therefore "ei" before "dad" is masculine.

Dyma'r plant (y) cafodd eu tad ei ladd. Here are the children whose father was killed.

The antecedent is "plant" therefore "eu" before "tad" is plural.

The negative form of "y/yr" is "na/nad" (the same as the negative form of "a". See page 77). Note that this "na" also is usually omitted in speech, although the mutations, aspirate to verbs beginning with c, p, t and soft to verbs beginning with g, b, d, ll, m, rh, remain.

e.g. Dyma'r bachgen na chafodd ei dad (ddim o'i) ei ladd.

Here's the boy whose father was not killed.

Note the location of the negative element "ddim". Note also the use of "o" (see page 38).

4 When the relative pronoun is dependent upon a preposition (e.g. in which/from which/ under which, etc.), "y/yr" is used, followed by the verb, subject and then the preposition, with the preposition referring back to the antecedent.

e.g. Dyma'r tŷ (y) mae e'n byw ynddo. Here's the house in which he lives.
Dyma'r ffatri (y) byddwch chi'n gweithio ynddi.

Here's the factory in which you will be be working.

The "y/yr" is usually omitted in speech.

The negative form of "y/yr" is "na/nad". Again "na" is usually omitted in speech although the mutations it causes remain.

e.g. Dyna'r fenyw roioch chi ddim o'r llythyr   That is the woman to whom you didn't
     iddi hi.   give the letter.

5 When the relative clause is adverbial in meaning the relative pronoun is translated by "y/yr". In speech however, "y/yr" is usually omitted. Note that the relative particle "y" does not cause mutation.

e.g. Dyma'r fan (y) cwympodd hi.   Here's the place where she fell.

    Rydw i'n cofio'r amser (y) buodd eich   I remember the time when your father
    tad chi farw.   died.

    Rydw i'n gwybod y ffordd (y) daethoch   I know the way that you came.
    chi.

The negative form of "y/yr" is "na/nad". Again "na/nad" is usually omitted in speech although the mutation it causes remains.

6 "Piau" is the relative form of the verb "Bod" meaning "to whom belongs, whose is/ are, who/which owns". The mutated form "biau" is generally used, with "sy" optional.

e.g. **Dyma'r bachgen (sy) biau'r llyfr.**   Here's the boy who owns the book.

In tenses other than the Present Tense, the third person singular forms of "Bod" are used with "Piau" to convey the tense meaning.

e.g. Siaradais i â'r dyn oedd biau'r tŷ.   I spoke to the man who owned the
                                              house.

"Piau" is frequently used after Pwy? (Who?).

e.g. **Pwy (sy) biau'r ci yma?**   Who owns this dog?

Similarly:

Pwy oedd biau'r bwthyn?   Who owned the cottage?

Pwy fydd biau'r fferm mewn deng mlynedd?   Who will own the farm in ten years?

The negative form of "biau" is "sy ddim biau" (who doesn't own).

e.g. Oes rhywun yma sy ddim biau beic?   Is there anyone here who doesn't own
                                              a bike?

Similarly:

. . .oedd ddim biau (who didn't own)
. . . fydd ddim biau (who will not own)

ADVERBIAL CLAUSES

An adverbial clause modifies the action of a verb, i.e. it tells how, why, when, where or to what extent an action takes place.

Adverbial clauses are always introduced by link words and fall into three categories:

A. ADVERBIAL CLAUSES—Introduced by certain link words and inflected tenses of the verb (or an inflected form of the verb "Bod" when used as an auxiliary).

Affirmative Clauses

1 **Pan (when)** (followed by soft mutation)
   e.g. Roeddwn i yn y tŷ pan ddaeth e.   I was in the house when he came.

2 **Tra (while)**

   e.g. Galwodd Gareth tra oeddet ti yn dref.   Gareth called while you were in town.
        Cwrddais i â Mair tra oeddwn i'n siopa   I met Mair while I was shopping
        ddoe.   yesterday.

Note that "pan" and "tra" are followed directly by the verb without the particle "y".

Note also that the forms of the third person of the verb "Bod" in the Present Tense commonly used after "pan" and "tra" are "mae" (sing.) and "maen" (pl.).

   e.g. Rydw i'n mynd i'r stafell wely i ddarllen   I'm going to the bedroom to read
        tra mae'r rhaglen yma ar y teledu.   while this programme is on the television.

3 **Fel (y) (as, at the time that, so that)**

   e.g.

Does neb yma fel (y) dywedais i.   There is nobody here as I said.
Fel roeddwn i'n cyrraedd yr ysgol y bore   As/At the time that I was arriving at
   yma gwelais i'r prifathro.   school this morning I saw the headmaster.

Ewch nawr fel (y) byddwch chi yna mewn   Go now so that you will be there in
   pryd.   time.

The particle "y" is usually omitted in speech.

4 **Achos (because)**

   e.g.

Dydw i ddim yn mynd i weld y gêm achos   I am not going to see the game because
   mae hi'n bwrw glaw.   it's raining.
Es i ddim i'r ysgol ddoe achos roedd annwyd   I didn't go to school yesterday because
   arna i.   I had a cold.

5 (Hyd)nes (y) (until)

e.g.

Peidiwch mynd allan i chwarae (hyd) nes (y) byddwch chi wedi gorffen eich gwaith cartref.

Don't go out to play until you have finished your homework.

6 Efallai (+ "y/yr") (perhaps)

(*a*) *to express the future*

Efallai (+ "y/yr") + Future Tense of "Bod" or the inflected form of the Future Tense.

e.g. Efallai (y) bydda i'n hwyr.

Perhaps I will be late.

Efallai (y) cewch chi wahoddiad i'r parti.

Perhaps you will receive an invitation to the party.

(*b*) *to express the conditional*

Efallai (+ "y/yr") + Conditional Tense.

e.g. Efallai (y) basai'n well i chi aros yn y gwely.

Perhaps it would be better for you to stay in bed.

Efallai (yr) hoffech chi ddod gyda fi.

Perhaps you would like to come with me.

7 Lle (y)/ble (y) (where)

e.g.

Eisteddwch lle (y)/ble (y) mynnwch.

Sit where you wish.

8 Os (if) with verbs in all tenses except the conditional tenses

e.g. Os ydych chi'n dod, dewch yn gynnar.

If you're coming, come early.

Peidiwch mynd allan os oes annwyd arnoch chi.

Don't go out if you've got a cold.

Gofynnwch iddo fe os ydy'r plant yn chwarae.

Ask him if the children are playing.

Note that "os" cannot be followed by "mae". It is followed by "oes" when the subject is indefinite, e.g. "annwyd" and by "ydy", when the subject is definite, e.g. "y plant" (as shown in the above examples).

Os ydy e wedi brifo'i goes, fydd e ddim yn gallu chwarae.

If he has hurt his leg, he won't be able to play.

Mae e'n siŵr o ddod os addawodd e.

He's sure to come if he promised.

9 Pe (if) + Imperfect Subjunctive or Pluperfect Tense

e.g. Pe baswn/bawn i wedi bod yn rhedeg, basech chi wedi colli'r ras.

If I had been running, you would have lost the race.

Pe baswn/bawn i'n gyfoethog, baswn i'n prynu tŷ mawr yn y dref.

If I were rich, I would buy a big house in the town.

This is one of the rare occasions when the subjunctive is still used after "pe".

Note that two forms of the subjunctive can occur after "pe". "Pe bawn i" is a special form restricted to the subjunctive, whereas "pe baswn i" which has an identical meaning, is also used to convey the ordinary conditional tense.

The difference conveyed by the subjunctive form is the same as the difference between "were" and "was" in English, e.g. in the sense that "were" is used in the following sentences:

I would go if I were ill.

If he were here now, he would tell you.

Negative Forms

There are two constructions after these conjunctions:

(a) In speech the most common construction is the inflected form of the verb (with soft mutation of verbs beginning with b, d, g, ll, rh, m, and aspirate mutation of verbs beginning with c, p, t)+ "ddim". These mutations have been caused by the negative particle "na/nad" which has disappeared, although the "d" of "nad" is still found with "dydw i", "doeddwn i", etc.

1 Pan

Pan ddaeth e ddim adre'n gynnar, es i i chwilio amdano fe.

When he didn't come home early, I went to look for him.

2 Tra

Aeth hi allan i ddodi'r dillad ar y lein tra doedd hi ddim yn bwrw glaw.

She went out to put the clothes on the line while it wasn't raining.

Tra doeddet ti ddim yn y tŷ gorffennais i'r peintio.

While you weren't in the house I finished the painting.

3 Fel

Ewch yn ddigon cynnar fel fyddwch chi ddim yn hwyr y tro yma.

Go early enough so that you won't be late this time.

4 Achos

Fyddwn ni ddim yn mynd i'r cyfandir yn yr haf achos does dim digon o arian gyda ni.

We won't be going to the continent in the summer because we haven't got enough money.

Mae e'n grac achos chafodd e ddim gwahoddiad i'r parti.

He is annoyed because he didn't have an invitation to the party.

5 (Hyd) nes

Bwytwch (hyd) nes fyddwch chi ddim yn gallu bwyta dim rhagor.

Eat until you can't eat any more.

6 Efallai

Efallai chewch chi ddim gwahoddiad i'r parti wedi'r cwbl.

Perhaps you won't have an invitation to the party after all.

Efallai fasech chi ddim eisiau dod beth bynnag.

Perhaps you wouldn't want to come anyway.

7 Lle/ble

Peidiwch mynd lle/ble dydych chi ddim wedi bod o'r blaen.

Don't go where you haven't been before.

8 Os

Os dydych chi ddim eisiau dod, dywedwch nawr.

If you don't want to come, say now.

Fydda i ddim yn mynd i'r disgo os fydda i ddim wedi cael ffrog newydd

I will not be going to the disco if I won't have had a new dress.

Ffoniff e ddim os fydd e ddim wedi bod yn llwyddiannus.

He won't phone if he won't have been successful.

9 Pe

Pe baswn i ddim mor dew baswn i'n gallu gwisgo'ch ffrog chi.

If I weren't so fat I would be able to wear your dress.

Note that "baswn i/bawn i" etc., does not undergo soft mutation in the negative form after "pe".

(b) An alternative negative form is expressed by "na" or "nad" + inflected form of the verb (with soft mutation of verbs beginning with b, d, g, ll, rh, m and aspirate mutation of verbs beginning with p, t, c after "na") + "ddim" (optional).

Pan na ddaeth e (ddim) adre'n gynnar, es i chwilio amdano fe.

Aeth e allan i ddodi'r dillad ar y lein tra nad oedd hi (ddim) yn bwrw glaw.

Tra nad oeddet ti (ddim) yn y tŷ gorffennais i'r peintio.

Ewch yn ddigon cynnar fel na fyddwch chi (ddim) yn hwyr y tro yma.

Bwytwch (hyd) nes na fyddwch chi (ddim) yn gallu bwyta dim rhagor.

Efallai na fasech chi (ddim) eisiau dod beth bynnag.

Peidiwch mynd lle/ble nad ydych chi (ddim) wedi bod o'r blaen.

Os nad ydych chi (ddim) eisiau dod, dywedwch nawr.

Bydda i'n mynd os na fydda i (ddim) yn rhy hwyr yn cyrraedd adre.

Pe na baswn i (ddim) mor dew, baswn i'n gallu gwisgo'ch ffrog chi.

B. ADVERBIAL CLAUSES INTRODUCED BY A CONJUNCTION + "BOD".

Affirmative Clauses

1 Er (although)

e.g. Er bod y dyn yn byw ymhell o'i waith, mae e'n cerdded yna bob dydd.

Although the man lives far from his work, he walks there every day.

Similarly:

Er bod y bachgen wedi mynd i'r gwely, dydy e ddim yn cysgu.

Although the boy has gone to bed, he is not sleeping.

When the subject is a pronoun, the appropriate form of the prefixed pronoun ("fy", "dy", "ei", etc.) is placed before "Bod" and the appropriate form of the affixed pronoun ("i, di, e", etc.) is placed after "Bod".

e.g. Daeth yr athrawes i'r ysgol er ei bod hi'n dost.

The teacher came to the school although she was ill.

Similarly:

Es i ddim i'r briodas er fy mod i wedi cael gwahoddiad.

I didn't go to the wedding although I had received an invitation.

2 Cyn (before)

e.g. Peidiwch mynd adre cyn bod y gloch yn canu.

Don't go home before the bell rings.

Roedd e wedi cyrraedd cyn bod y cloc wedi taro deg.

He had arrived before the clock had struck ten.

3 Cyhyd â (as long as)

e.g. Does dim gwahaniaeth beth fydd y canlyniad cyhyd â'i fod e'n gwneud ei orau.

It doesn't matter what the result will be as long as he does his best.

4 Achos (because)

Learners will find that the simplest way of learning "achos" is the one described in Section A on page 81. However, "achos" can also be used in the following manner.

(*a*) When the tense of the clause in English is the Present or Past Continuous, the clause in Welsh is introduced by achos + bod + subject + yn . . .

e.g. Rydw i'n mynd i Gaerdydd heno achos bod Cymru'n chwarae pêl-droed yn Yr Eidal.

I am going to Cardiff tonight because Wales are playing football against Italy.

Note the use of the prefixed and affixed pronouns in the following example.

Dydy e ddim yn dod achos ei fod e eisiau gwneud ei waith cartref.

He isn't coming because he wants to do his homework.

(*b*) Subordinate clauses in the Past or Perfect Tense can be **introduced either as** explained on page 81 or by achos + bod + subject + wedi . . .

e.g. Roedd y dyrfa'n gweiddi achos bod Cymru wedi ennill.

The crowd was shouting because Wales had won.

Similarly:

Arhosodd Aled adre achos ei fod e wedi cael annwyd.

Aled stayed at home because he had had a cold.

4 Efallai (perhaps)

Efallai + "Bod" is used when the verb is in the Present or Perfect Tense.

e.g.

Efallai bod y siop ar agor.

Perhaps the shop is open.

Efallai eu bod nhw wedi colli'r bws.

Perhaps they have missed the bus.

5 Am, Gan (since)

e.g.

Enillodd Gwen y wobr gynta am ei bod hi wedi canu mor dda.

Gwen won the first prize since she had sung so well.

Dyweda i wrthoch chi gan eich bod chi'n gofyn.

I'll tell you since you ask.

6 Rhag ofn (in case)

e.g.

Peidiwch prynu un rhag ofn bod Mair wedi prynu'r un peth.

Don't buy one in case Mary has bought the same thing.

84

Negative Forms

In speech the most common form is expressed by the affirmative construction + "ddim".

e.g. Er bod y tywydd ddim yn dda, rydw i'n mynd allan.

Although the weather isn't good, I am going out.

Roedd pawb yn drist achos bod Cymru ddim wedi ennill.

Everyone was sad because Wales hadn't won.

Efallai bod y siop ddim ar gau wedi'r cwbl.

Perhaps the shop isn't closed after all.

Collodd hi'r bws am ei bod hi ddim wrth yr arhosfan mewn pryd.

She missed the bus since she wasn't at the bus stop in time.

Gan eich bod chi ddim wedi bod yng Nghaernarfon erioed, hoffech chi fynd yna gyda fi?

Since you have never been to Caernarfon, would you like to go there with me?

Peidiwch dweud wrth Non rhag ofn ei bod hi ddim yn gwybod.

Don't tell Non in case she doesn't know.

An alternative negative form is expressed by "na/nad" + inflected form of the verb (+ "ddim" optional).

e.g. Er nad ydy'r tywydd (ddim) yn dda rydw i'n mynd allan.

Although the weather isn't good I am going out.

Roedd pawb yn drist achos nad oedd Cymru (ddim) wedi ennill.

Everyone was sad because Wales hadn't won.

Efallai nad ydy'r siop (ddim) ar gau wedi'r cwbl.

Perhaps the shop isn't closed after all.

Am nad oedd e (ddim) yn gallu defnyddio cyfrifiadur, chafodd e ddim o'r swydd.

Since he couldn't use a computer, he didn't get the job.

Gan nad ydy hi (ddim) yn bwrw glaw rydw i'n mynd allan am dro.

Since it isn't raining I am going out for a walk.

Peidiwch addo rhag ofn na fyddwch chi (ddim) yn gallu dod wedi'r cwbl.

Don't promise in case you won't be able to come after all.

C. ADVERBIAL CLAUSES INTRODUCED BY A CONJUNCTION, THE PREPOSITION "I" + VERB-NOUN.

The subject is placed after the preposition "i".

1 Er mwyn (in order to/that)
e.g.

Codais i'n gynnar y bore yma er mwyn i'r bechgyn ddal y bws.	I got up early this morning in order that the boys might catch the bus.
Aberthodd y rhieni bopeth er mwyn i'r plant gael gwell cyfle.	The parents sacrificed everything in order that the children should have a better opportunity.

2 Wedi (after)
e.g.

Roedd y tŷ'n wag wedi i bawb adael.	The house was empty after everyone had left.

3 Ar ôl (after)
e.g.

Roedd pobman yn dawel ar ôl i'r plant fynd i'r gwely.	Everywhere was quiet after the children had gone to bed.

4 Erbyn (by (the time that))
e.g.

Roedd hi'n nosi erbyn iddo fe gyrraedd.	It was getting dark by the time (that) he arrived.

5 Wrth (as, at the time that)
e.g.

Gwelais i ddamwain wrth i fi fynd adre neithiwr.	I saw an accident as I was going home last night.

6 Er (although)
e.g.

Rydw i bron llwgu er i fi gael cinio ychydig o amser yn ôl.	I am nearly starving although I had dinner a short time ago.

7 Cyn (before)
e.g.

Cymerwch gwpanaid o de cyn i chi fynd.	Have a cup of tea before you go.

8 **Rhag ofn (in case)**

e.g.

Paid rhedeg rhag ofn i ti gwympo.　　　Don't run in case you fall.

9 **(Hyd) nes (until)**

e.g.

Arhosais i yn y gwely (hyd) nes i Mam　　I stayed in bed until my mother called
alw arna i.　　　me.

10 **Heb (without)**

Peidiwch mynd i mewn i'r adeilad heb i chi　Don't go into the building without
gael caniatâd.　　　having permission.

Note that the tense of the verb in the subordinate clause is determined by the tense of the verb in the main clause.

It will be seen that there are three ways of forming adverbial clauses. Some of the link words used to introduce these clauses can be followed by more than one of the adverbial constructions.

Link word	*Construction*	
achos	A.	B.
(hyd) nes	A.	C.
efallai	A.	B.
er	B.	C.
cyn	B.	C.
rhag ofn	B.	C.

NOUN CLAUSES

A noun clause in English is often introduced by the declarative "that".

e.g. I know that John is coming.

However, "that" is sometimes omitted in English, although its meaning is generally understood.

e.g. I know John is coming.

The relative pronoun "that" is also omitted sometimes in English.

e.g. I have lost the present (that) you gave me.

These are the only two "thats" which may be omitted in English.

It is important that the relative pronoun "that" and the declarative "that" should not be confused.

A simple test may be undertaken to decide which of these two "thats" should be used. If "that" can be replaced by "which" or "who", the relative pronoun should be used to introduce the relative clause.

e.g. Here is the dog that/which bit me.

The man who/that called to see us was my father's friend.

If it is impossible to substitute "which" or "who" for "that", then the declarative "that" should be used.

e.g. The man said that he had called to see us.

It is impossible to say "The man said which . . .", therefore, it must be the declarative "that".

The noun clause is expressed in Welsh as follows:

1 The Future or Conditional Tense

(1) *The Affirmative Form*

e.g. Rydw i'n gwybod (y) bydd hi'n cyrraedd yfory.

I know that she will be arriving to-morrow.

Dywedodd e (yr) hoffai fe brynu tŷ yn y wlad.

He said that he would like to buy a house in the country.

Rydw i'n meddwl (y) caiff e gar newydd y flwyddyn nesa.

I think that he will have a new car next year.

Note that "y/yr" is usually omitted in speech.

(2) *The Negative Form*

In speech, the most common method is formed by adding "ddim" to the affirmative construction.

e.g. Rydw i'n gwybod fydd hi ddim yn cyrraedd yfory.

I know that she will not be arriving tomorrow.

Dywedodd e fasai fe ddim yn prynu tŷ yn y wlad.

He said that he wouldn't buy a house in the country.

Note that the verb undergoes mutation at the beginning of the noun clause.
This is caused by the negative particle "na" which is no longer used to introduce the negative clause. "Na" causes *aspirate mutation* to words beginning with p, t, c, and *soft mutation* to words beginning with b, d, g, ll, rh, m. This mutation remains even when the particle "na" is no longer used.

An alternative negative form is expressed by:

"na" (before consonants)/"nad" (before vowels) + inflected tense of verb(+ "ddim" optional).

Note

"Na" causes (*a*) aspirate mutation to p, t, c.
            (*b*) soft mutation to b, d, g, ll, rh, m.

e.g. Rydw i'n siŵr na thalodd e (ddim) am y tocyn.	I am sure that he didn't pay for the ticket.
Rydw i'n gwybod na fydd hi (ddim) yn cyrraedd yfory.	I know that she won't be arriving tomorrow.

2 However, if the verb in the subordinate clause utilises the Present or Imperfect Tense of "Bod", i.e. "rydw i", etc., or "roeddwn i", etc., the construction is different.

(1) The Affirmative Form

(*a*) When the subject is a noun, the verb changes to "Bod".

e.g. Mae'r plant yn hwyr.	The children are late.
Mae'r prifathro'n gwybod bod y plant yn hwyr.	The headmaster knows the children are late.
Roedd y plant yn hwyr.	The children were late.
Roedd y prifathro'n gwybod bod y plant yn hwyr.	The headmaster knew the children were late.

Similarly:

Mae'r wraig yn byw mewn bwthyn.	The woman lives in a cottage.
Rydw i'n meddwl bod y wraig yn byw mewn bwthyn.	I think the woman lives in a cottage.
Mae'r teledu'n gweithio nawr.	The television is working now.
Rydyn ni'n gweld bod y teledu'n gweithio nawr.	We see that the television is working now.
Mae'r plant yma'n swnllyd.	These children are noisy.
Rydw i'n deall bod y plant yma'n swnllyd.	I understand these children are noisy.
Roedd Gwyn yn dweud y gwir.	Gwyn was telling the truth.
Doedd e ddim yn credu bod Gwyn yn dweud y gwir.	He didn't believe Gwyn was telling the truth.
Roedd y merched ar y trên.	The girls were on the train.
Roedd Mr. Evans yn siŵr bod y merched ar y trên.	Mr. Evans was sure the girls were on the train.
Roedd Siân yn y disgo neithiwr.	Siân was in the disco last night.
Roeddwn i'n meddwl bod Siân yn y disgo neithiwr.	I thought Siân was in the disco last night.

Note that "Bod" changes to "Fod" when it is the direct object of the inflected form of the verb in the main clause:

e.g. Dywedodd yr athro fod Gareth wedi
colli'r bws adre.

The teacher said that Gareth had missed the bus home.

(b) With a pronoun subject, the appropriate form of the prefixed pronoun ("fy, dy", etc.), is placed before "Bod", and the corresponding form of the affixed pronoun ("i, di", etc.) after "Bod".

e.g. Roedd e'n dost.
Dywedodd hi ei fod e'n dost.

He was ill.
She said he was ill.

Similarly:

Rydych chi'n gallu dod.	You are able to come.
Rydw i'n gobeithio eich bod chi'n gallu dod.	I hope you are able to come.
Rydyn ni'n byw yma.	We live here.
Clywodd e ein bod ni'n byw yma.	He heard we live here.
Maen nhw'n hapus.	They are happy.
Mae e'n gweld eu bod nhw'n hapus.	He sees they are happy.
Roeddwn i'n brysur.	I was busy.
Roedd e'n gwybod fy mod i'n brysur.	He knew I was busy.
Roedd hi'n mynd i ffwrdd ddoe.	She was going away yesterday.
Deallais i ei bod hi'n mynd i ffwrdd ddoe.	I understood she was going away yesterday.
Roedd e'n cystadlu ddoe.	He was competing yesterday.
Roeddwn i'n falch ei fod e'n cystadlu ddoe.	I was glad he was competing yesterday.

(2) The Negative Form

In speech the negative is usually formed by adding "ddim" to the affirmative construction.

e.g. Mae'r pennaeth yn gwybod bod y plant
ddim yma.

The headteacher knows the children are not here.

Roedd e'n gwybod fy mod i ddim yn
brysur.

He knew I wasn't busy.

An alternative negative form used mainly in literary Welsh is expressed by "na/nad" + inflected tense (+ "ddim" optional).

e.g. Rydw i'n gwybod nad ydy e (ddim) yn
dod.

I know he isn't coming.

Dywedon nhw nad oedd John (ddim) yn
teimlo'n dda.

They said John wasn't feeling well.

Dywedodd e na chlywodd e (ddim)
erioed y fath ganu.

He said that he had never heard such singing.

3 The Past Tense

The following constructions are used to express the Past Tense in a noun clause:

(A) The first of these constructions is normally used in speech in South Wales to express the Past Tense. The verb is regarded as if it were in the Perfect Tense and becomes "bod" and "wedi".

(1) The Affirmative Form

e.g. Aeth y trên.	The train went.
Rydw i'n siŵr bod y trên wedi mynd.	I'm sure the train has gone.
Gwelais i'r bachgen ddoe.	I saw the boy yesterday.
Rydw i'n meddwl fy mod i wedi gweld y bachgen ddoe.	I think I saw the boy yesterday.
Cerddon nhw adre neithiwr.	They walked home last night.
Dywedodd e eu bod nhw wedi cerdded adre neithiwr.	He said they walked home last night.

(2) The Negative Form

. . . bod . . . ddim wedi . . .

e.g. Rydw i'n siwr bod y trên ddim wedi mynd.	I'm sure the train hasn't gone.

(B) The preposition "i" + subject + verb-noun with soft mutation. This construction is found mainly in literary Welsh.

(1) The Affirmative Form

e.g. Aeth y bws yn gynnar.	The bus went early.
Rydw i'n siŵr i'r bws fynd yn gynnar.	I'm sure the bus went early.
Rhedodd y bachgen i'r siop.	The boy ran to the shop.
Meddyliais i i'r bachgen redeg i'r siop.	I thought the boy ran to the shop.
Canodd y plant yn dda.	The children sang well.
Rydw i'n credu i'r plant ganu'n dda.	I believe the children sang well.

When the subject is a pronoun, the appropriate forms of "i" ("i fi, i ti, iddo fe", etc.) are used.

e.g. Aeth e'n gynnar.	He/It went early.
Rydw i'n siŵr iddo fe fynd yn gynnar.	I'm sure he/it went early.

(2) The Negative Form

"na/nad" + inflected form of the Past Tense (+ "ddim" optional).

e.g. Rydw i'n deall nad aeth y ferch (ddim) yn gynnar.	I understand the girl didn't go early.

(C) In NorthWales the verb "ddaru" + "i" + subject + verb-noun with soft mutation are used to express the Past Tense in Welsh.

(1) The Affirmative Form

e.g. Rydw i'n siŵr ddaru i John fynd.   I'm sure John went.

When the subject is a pronoun, the appropriate forms of "i" ("i fi, i ti, iddo fe", etc.) are used.

e.g. Rydw i'n meddwl ddaru iddo fe fynd.   I think he went.

(2) The Negative Form

The most common form is the affirmative construction + "ddim".

e.g. Rydw i'n gwybod ddaru iddo fe ddim   I know he didn't go.
       mynd.

Note

1 An emphatic sentence (see page 72) becomes an emphatic noun clause by using the link word "mai/taw".

(1) The Affirmative Form

e.g. Rydw i'n siŵr mai/taw Gareth sy'n byw   I'm sure *Gareth* lives here.
       yma.

Roedd e'n gwybod mai/taw fi ddaeth   He knew *I* had brought the present.
â'r anrheg.

(2) The Negative Form

In speech the most common form is the affirmative construction + "dim".

e.g. Rydw i'n siŵr mai/taw dim Gareth sy'n   I'm sure *Gareth* doesn't live here.
       byw yma.
Roedd e'n gwybod mai/taw dim fi ddaeth   He knew it wasn't *I* who brought the
â'r anrheg.   present.

An alternative negative form is expressed by "nad" (instead of "mai/taw dim").

e.g. Rydw i'n siŵr nad Gareth sy'n byw yma.
       Roedd e'n gwybod nad fi ddaeth â'r anrheg.

The construction is found mainly in literary Welsh.

2 Noun clauses can occur in circumstances other than as objects of verbs. They can follow idomatic phrases expressing emotion, e.g. "Mae'n ddrwg gyda fi" (I'm sorry); "Mae'n dda gyda fi" (I'm glad/pleased); "Mae rhaid i fi" (I must) etc. and some impersonal expressions, e.g. "Mae'n rhyfedd" (It's strange); "Mae'n siŵr" (It's sure); "Mae'n amlwg" (It's evident), etc.

e.g. Mae'n ddrwg gyda fi bod Gwyn yn dost.   I'm sorry Gwyn is ill.
Mae'n rhyfedd ei fod e'n hwyr.   It's strange he's late.

3 The dependent question, introduced in English by "whether" has the same form in Welsh as the direct question and is introduced by "a".

e.g. Gofynnodd i fi (a) oeddwn i'n dost.   He asked me if (whether) I was ill.

This "a" is usually omitted in speech.

Note that the use of "os", which is often confused with the conjunction "a" in these circumstances, is strictly speaking incorrect and should be avoided.

(After "a" the verb in the third person singular Present Tense must be "oes" or "ydy".

e.g.   Gofynnwch (a) oes siwgr ar y bwrdd.   Ask whether there's any sugar on the table.

Tybed (a) ydy John yn dod?   I wonder whether John's coming?)

QUESTIONS AND ANSWERS

1 Questions that begin with verbs have verb forms as answers. The verb forms used in the answers depend upon the persons to whom the questions are asked.

PRESENT TENSE

e.g. Ydych chi'n byw yng Nghaerdydd?   Do you live in Cardiff?
Ydw (rydw i'n byw yng Nghaerdydd).   Yes (I live in Cardiff).
Nag ydw (dydw i ddim yn byw yng Nghaerdydd).   No (I don't live in Cardiff).

The answers above are used if one person is answering the questions.

Ydyn (rydyn ni'n byw yng Nghaerdydd).   Yes (we live in Cardiff).
Nag ydyn (dydyn ni ddim yn byw yng Nghaerdydd).   No (we don't live in Cardiff).

The answers above are used if more than one person is involved in the answer.

Ydyn nhw'n hapus?   Are they happy?
Ydyn (maen nhw'n hapus).   Yes (they are happy).
Nag ydyn (dydyn nhw ddim yn hapus).   No (they aren't happy).

Note: Ydy and Oes

"Mae" changes to "Ydy" in the interrogative when the subject is definite.

e.g. Mae Alun yn yr ysgol.   Alun is in school.
Ydy Alun yn yr ysgol?   Is Alun in school?
Ydy (mae Alun yn yr ysgol).   Yes (Alun is in school).
Nag ydy (dydy Alun ddim yn yr ysgol).   No (Alun isn't in school).
Mae'r bachgen yn dal.   The boy is tall.
Ydy'r bachgen yn dal?   Is the boy tall?
Ydy (mae'r bachgen yn dal).   Yes (the boy is tall).
Nag ydy (dydy'r bachgen ddim yn dal).   No (the boy isn't tall).

Note that "Ydyn" (yes) and "Nag ydyn" (no) are used when the subject is plural.

e.g. Ydy'r bechgyn yma?   Are the boys here?
    Ydyn (mae'r bechgyn yma).   Yes (the boys are here).
    Nag ydyn (dydy'r bechgyn ddim yma). No (the boys aren't here).

"Mae" changes to "Oes" in the interrogative when the subject is indefinite.

e.g. Mae te yn y tebot.   There is tea in the teapot.
    Oes te yn y tebot?   Is there tea in the teapot?
    Oes (mae te yn y tebot).   Yes (there is tea in the teapot).
    Nag oes (does dim te yn y tebot). No (there isn't any tea in the teapot).

Note that if a question begins with "Oes" then "Oes" must be used in the answer.

"Dim" always precedes the subject in a negative sentence when the subject is indefinite.

e.g. Doedd dim te yn y siop.   There wasn't any tea in the shop.
    (Imperfect Tense)
    Fydd dim te yn y siop.   There won't be any tea in the shop.
    (Future Tense)

IMPERFECT TENSE

e.g. Oedd e'n chwarae ddoe?   Was he playing yesterday?
    Oedd (roedd e'n chwarae ddoe).   Yes (he was playing yesterday).
    Nag oedd (doedd e ddim yn chwarae   No (he wasn't playing yesterday).
    ddoe).

FUTURE TENSE 1

e.g. Fyddi di ar y bws yn y bore?   Will you be on the bus in the morning?
    Bydda (bydda i ar y bws yn y bore). Yes (I will be on the bus in the morning).

    Na fydda (fydda i ddim ar y bws yn y No (I won't be on the bus in the morning).
    bore).

CONDITIONAL TENSE

e.g. Fasai hi'n dod?   Would she come?
    Basai (basai hi'n dod).   Yes (she would come).
    Na fasai (fasai hi ddim yn dod).   No (she wouldn't come).

Alternative Form

e.g. Fyddai fe'n mynd?	Would he go?
Byddai (byddai fe'n mynd).	Yes (he would go).
Na fyddai (fyddai fe ddim yn mynd).	No (he wouldn't go).

FUTURE TENSE 2

e.g. Ganwch chi yn y cyngerdd?	Will you sing in the concert?
Gwna (cana i yn y cyngerdd).	Yes (I will sing in the concert).
Na wna (chana i ddim yn y cyngerdd).	No (I will not sing in the concert).

The appropriate person of the inflected Future Tense of the auxiliary verb "gwneud" (to do) is used in most cases to answer questions in this category.

But with the following verbs where the tense conveys the present rather than the future, the verb forms are used to answer questions: "gallu/medru" (to be able to), "gwybod" (to know), "gweld" (to see), although this usage is becoming less common with "gwybod" and "gweld" by now.

e.g. Allwch chi ddod?	Can you come?
Galla (galla i ddod).	Yes (I can come).
Na alla (alla i ddim dod).	No (I can't come).
Fedrwch chi weld y car?	Can you see the car?
Medra (medra i weld y car).	Yes (I can see the car).
Na fedra (fedra i ddim gweld y car).	No (I can't see the car).

It is, of course, possible with these verbs to use the long form of the Present Tense.

e.g. Ydych chi'n gallu/medru dod?	Can you come?
Ydw.	Yes.
Nag ydw.	No.

2 Questions that begin with a verb in the Past Tense (short form) have "Do" (yes) and "Naddo" (no) as answers, irrespective of the person of the verb.

e.g. Fuoch chi allan?	Did you go out?
Do (bues i allan).	Yes (I went out).
Naddo (fues i ddim allan).	No (I didn't go out).
Welodd e'r gêm?	Did he see the game?
Do (gwelodd e'r gêm).	Yes (he saw the game).
Naddo (welodd e ddim o'r gêm).	No (he didn't see the game).
Ganon nhw'n dda?	Did they sing well?
Do (canon nhw'n dda).	Yes (they sang well).
Naddo (chanon nhw ddim yn dda).	No (they didn't sing well).

3 Questions which do not begin with a verb have "Ie" (yes) and "Nage" (no) as answers.

e.g. Yn y tŷ mae John?	Is John *in the house*?
Ie (yn y tŷ mae John).	Yes (John is *in the house*).
Nage (dim yn y tŷ mae John).	No (John isn't *in the house*).

Siopwr ydy Mr. Edwards?	Is Mr. Edwards a *shopkeeper*?
Ie (siopwr ydy Mr. Edwards)	Yes (Mr. Edwards is a *shopkeeper*).
Nage (dim siopwr ydy Mr. Edwards).	No (Mr. Edwards isn't a *shopkeeper*).

Gwilym sy yn y tŷ?	Is it *Gwilym* who's in the house?
Ie (Gwilym sy yn y tŷ).	Yes (it's *Gwilym* who's in the house).
Nage (dim Gwilym sy yn y tŷ).	No (it isn't *Gwilym* who's in the house).

e.g. Dydd Llun oedd hi ddoe?	Was it *Monday* yesterday?
Ie (dydd Llun oedd hi ddoe).	Yes (it was *Monday* yesterday).
Nage (dim dydd Llun oedd hi ddoe).	No (it wasn't *Monday* yesterday).

In literary Welsh "nid" is used instead of "dim" in the negative.

e.g. Nage (nid dydd Llun oedd hi ddoe).

Note that the above sections do not include information questions i.e. questions that begin with interrogative adverbs, pronouns and adjectives e.g. Ble? Pam? Sut? Pryd? etc. Examples of such questions are given in the following section, together with model answers.

4 When the interrogative elements are used, three different relationships are possible with the verb. This can be seen most clearly when the verb involved is the verb "Bod" (to be) in the third person singular Present Tense. "Mae", "sy" or "ydy" are used in accordance with certain rules.

A Ble? (Where?); Pryd? (When?); Sut? (How?); Pam? (Why?)

1 When the verb "Bod" (to be) is involved in the third person singular Present Tense, the form needed is "mae".

Ble mae'r bachgen?	Where is the boy?
Mae'r bachgen yn y dref.	The boy is in the town.
Pryd mae e'n mynd ar ei wyliau?	When is he going on his holidays?
Mae e'n mynd ar ei wyliau dydd Sadwrn.	He is going on his holidays on Saturday.
Sut mae hi'n mynd i'r ddawns?	How is she going to the dance?
Mae hi'n mynd i'r ddawns ar y bws.	She's going to the dance on the bus.
Pam mae e'n mynd i Gaerdydd?	Why is he going to Cardiff?
Mae e'n mynd i Gaerdydd achos mae e eisiau gweld y gêm rygbi.	He's going to Cardiff because he wants to see the rugby game.

Note that "maen nhw" is the form used in the third person plural.

Sut maen nhw'n teimlo?	How are they feeling?
Maen nhw'n teimlo'n dost.	They are feeling ill.

2 If other forms of the verb "Bod" (to be) follow these interrogatives the "r" of "rydw i" etc. and "roeddwn i", etc. is retained and no mutation occurs to "baswn i" etc., "bydda i" etc. and "bues i" etc.

Ble rydych chi'n byw?	Where do you live?
Rydw i'n byw yng Nghaernarfon.	I live in Caernarfon.
Pryd roeddech chi yn y coleg?	When were you in college?
Roeddwn i yn y coleg pum mlynedd yn ôl.	I was in college five years ago.
Sut byddwn ni'n teithio?	How shall we be travelling?
Byddwn ni'n teithio yn y car.	We shall be travelling in the car.
Pam rydych chi'n gwisgo cot fawr?	Why are you wearing an overcoat?
Rydw i'n gwisgo cot fawr achos mae hi'n oer.	I'm wearing an overcoat because it's cold.

3 When the interrogatives are followed by inflected forms of the verb, no mutation occurs.

Ble gweloch chi Alun?	Where did you see Alun?
Gwelais i Alun yn y parti.	I saw Alun in the party.
Pryd prynodd e'r car?	When did he buy the car?
Prynodd e'r car dydd Gwener.	He bought the car on Friday.
Sut gyrrodd hi?	How did she drive?
Gyrrodd hi'n dda.	She drove well.
Pam prynodd hi ffrog newydd?	Why did she buy a new dress?
Prynodd hi ffrog newydd achos roedd hi'n mynd i ddawns yr ysgol.	She bought a new dress because she was going to the school dance.

B **Pwy? (Who?); Beth? (What?); Faint (o)? (How many?); Sawl/Sawl un? (How many?); Pa? (Which); P'un? (Which one); Pa rai? (Which ones?); Sut ? (What kind of?); Pa fath o? (What kind of?).**

When the verb "Bod" (to be) is involved in the third person singular Present Tense, the forms used are either "mae", "sy" or "ydy".

1 "Mae" is used when it is immediately followed by a noun or pronoun and a verb-noun with soft mutation to the verb-noun. The interrogative element in this instance is seeking to discover something about the act which the noun or pronoun following "mae" is performing.

e.g. Pwy mae John yn helpu?	Whom is John helping?
Mae John yn helpu ei ffrind.	John's helping his friend.

i.e. Who is receiving the act being done by John?

Beth mae e'n dorri?	What is he cutting?
Mae e'n torri'r glaswellt.	He is cutting the grass.
Faint o geir mae'r garej wedi werthu?	How many cars has the garage sold?
Mae'r garej wedi gwerthu un deg pedwar o geir.	The garage has sold fourteen cars.
Sawl cwpanaid o goffi mae hi wedi gael?	How many cups of coffee has she had?
Mae hi wedi cael dau gwpanaid o goffi.	She's had two cups of coffee.
P'un rydych chi wedi ddewis?	Which one have you chosen?
Rydw i wedi dewis yr un coch.	I've chosen the red one.
Pa gig maen nhw'n hoffi orau?	Which meat do they like best?
Maen nhw'n hoffi cig oen orau.	They like lamb best.
Pa rai roeddech chi eisiau?	Which ones did you want?
Roeddwn i eisiau'r rhai newydd.	I wanted the new ones.
Sut ⎱ lyfrau byddwch chi'n brynu i'r Pa fath o ⎰ Nadolig?	What kind of books will you be buying for Christmas?
Bydda i'n prynu llyfrau pêl-droed i'r Nadolig.	I shall be buying football books for Christmas.

Note that no mutation occurs to "baswn i" etc., "bydda i", etc., "bues i" ,etc. after these interrogatives.

2 "Sy" is used

(a) When it is followed immediately by "yn" + verb or "wedi" + verb.

Pwy sy'n mynd?	Who is going?
Mae Alun yn mynd.	Alun is going.
Beth sy wedi digwydd?	What has happened?
Mae'r bachgen wedi cwympo.	The boy has fallen.
Sawl un sy'n hoffi nofio?	How many like swimming?
Pedwar.	Four.
P'un sy wedi ennill y ras?	Which one has won the race?
Gwilym.	Gwilym.
Faint o blant sy'n dod i'r parti?	How many children are coming to the party?
Chwech.	Six.

(b) When it is followed by "yn" + adjective.

Pwy sy'n ddrwg?	Who's naughty?
Ann.	Ann.
Beth sy'n dda ar y teledu heno?	What's good on the television tonight?
Gêm rygbi.	A rugby match.
Sut gig sy'n dda i frecwast?	What sort of meat is good for breakfast?
Cig moch.	Bacon.
Pa storïau sy'n ddiddorol?	Which stories are interesting?
Storïau ditectif.	Detective stories.

(*c*) When it is followed by an adverb or adverbial phrase.

Pwy sy yma?	Who's here?
Mr. Roberts.	Mr. Roberts.
Beth sy yn y bocs?	What's in the box?
Llyfrau.	Books.
Faint o fechgyn sy yn y stafell?	How many boys are there in the room?
Un deg un.	Eleven.
Sawl plât sy ar y bwrdd?	How many plates are there on the table?
Tri.	Three.

(*d*) When it is followed by an indefinite noun. Note that "yn" must be placed before the noun.

Pwy sy'n athro?	Who's a teacher?
Mr. Edwards.	Mr. Edwards.
Faint o fenywod yng Nghymru sy'n athrawon?	How many women in Wales are teachers?
Llawer iawn.	Very many.
Sut berson sy'n llyfrgellydd?	What sort of person is a librarian?
Person trefnus.	An orderly person.
P'un o'r menywod sy'n ddoctor?	Which one of the women is a doctor?
Mrs. Jenkins.	Mrs. Jenkins.

With this usage, the verb can only be in the third person singular (e.g. "sy/oedd/fydd/fuodd/fasai") and undergoes soft mutation.

Pwy oedd yma?	Who was here?
Sawl merch fydd yn y parti?	How many girls will be in the party?
Beth fasai'n digwydd?	What would happen?

3 "Ydy" is used when the following word is a definite noun or pronoun and the sense is complete.

Pwy ydy hi?	Who is she?
Pwy ydy'r pennaeth?	Who is the headteacher?

When the pronoun following "ydy" is not in the third person singular, then the appropriate form of the verb is used.

e.g. Pwy ydw i?	Who am I?
Beth ydych chi?	What are you?

Note

The "r" of "rydw i, roeddwn i" etc. is dropped with this construction,

e.g. Beth ydych chi?	What are you?

Note also that the third person plural is "ydyn nhw".

e.g. Pwy ydyn nhw?	Who are they?

Finally soft mutation occurs.

e.g. Pwy fydd e?   Pwy fasai fe?

When, in this group, interrogatives are followed by inflected forms of the verb soft mutation occurs.

Pwy welodd e?	Who did he see?
Gwelodd e Catrin.	He saw Catrin.
Beth brynodd hi?	What did she buy?
Prynodd hi got newydd.	She bought a new coat.
Faint o arian gawson nhw ar y daith gerdded?	How much money did they have on the sponsored walk?
Deg punt.	Ten pounds.
Sut gar brynon nhw?	What sort of a car did they buy?
Car coch.	A red car.

Further Notes

1 This note will help to clarify the distinction between "Pwy mae . . .?" and "Pwy ydy . . .?"

(a) Pwy mae John/e yn ddilyn?   Whom is John/he following?

In this question "Pwy" does not refer to "John/e" but to the unknown person "John/e" is following i.e. the pronoun/noun following "mae" is not the one to which "Pwy" refers.

(b) Pwy ydy e?   Who is he?

In this question the "e" is known and we are being asked for additional information about him, such as his name, occupation or identification (in a group of others) i.e. the "Pwy" refers directly to the "e" following "ydy".

Beth ydy hwn?	What is this?
Bocs.	A box.
Sut ddyn ydy'r plismon newydd yn y pentref?	What sort of a man is the new policeman in the village?
Dyn tal.	A tall man.
Pa fath o afalau ydy'r rhain?	What kind of apples are these?
Afalau coginio.	Cooking apples.
P'un ydy Gareth?	Which one is Gareth?
Yr un gyda'r crys glas.	The one with the blue shirt.

2 The interrogative "Pa mor . . .?" (How . . .?) belongs to Group A when it is followed by a full verbal form.

e.g. Pa mor gyflym mae e'n mynd?   How fast does he go?
      Mae e'n mynd yn gyflym iawn.   He goes very fast.

When followed by a definite noun or pronoun it belongs to Group B.

e.g. Pa mor glyfar ydy hi?   How clever is she?
     Mae hi'n eitha clyfar.   She is quite clever.
     Pa mor dal ydy Phil?   How tall is Phil?
     Mae e'n rhy dal.   He is too tall.

Note that "Pa mor . . . ?" is always followed by an adjective which undergoes soft mutation (except ll, rh). It can never be followed by "sy".

3 The following rule will reveal whether the "r" in the forms of the verb "Bod" (to be) (e.g. "rydw i, roeddwn i" etc.) should be retained after the interrogatives.

If "mae" can be used after the interrogatives in the third person singular Present Tense, then the "r" in the forms of the verb "Bod" (to be) is retained.

e.g. Pryd mae e'n dod?   When is he coming?
     Pryd rydych chi'n dod?   When are you coming?
     Pryd roedd e'n dod?   When was he coming?

If "mae" cannot be used in these circumstances then the "r" is omitted.

e.g. Pwy ydy e?   Who is he?
     Pwy ydych chi?   Who are you?
     Pwy oedd hi?   Who was she?

Note also that when the "r" is retained, "maen nhw" is the form used in the third person plural.

e.g. Ble rydych chi'n byw?   Where do you live?
     Ble maen nhw'n byw?   Where do they live?

When the "r" is omitted, the form used in the third person plural is "ydyn nhw".

e.g. Pwy ydych chi?   Who are you?
     Pwy ydyn nhw?   Who are they?

When the form used after the interrogatives omits the "r", then soft mutation will occur in the following tenses—"baswn i" etc., "bydda i", etc., "bues i" etc.

e.g. Beth fasai'n digwydd?   What would happen?
     Pwy fydd yn dod?   Who will be coming?

Learners need not be over alarmed by the use of this "r" in "rydw i" etc. It is largely a matter for the eye and has no significance in speech.

4 The verb-noun following the verb "Bod" after an interrogative undergoes soft mutation.

e.g. Beth mae e'n ddarllen?   What is he reading?

This soft mutation is caused by a pronoun which has since disappeared in speech.
e.g. Beth mae'n (ei) ddarllen?

However, while there is no need to use the pronoun in this construction, some prefer to do so. In so doing an added difficulty occurs, since the pronoun used may be "ei" (m.), "ei" (f.), "eu" (pl.) and the appropriate mutation will have to be used.

e.g. Pa ferch rydych chi'n ei charu?   Which girl do you love?
     Pa lyfrau rydych chi'n eu darllen?   Which books do you read?

In view of this complication, it is better for learners to omit the pronoun and merely use the soft mutation. This would give: Pa ferch rydych chi'n garu? Pa lyfrau rydych chi'n ddarllen?

5 (a) Faint (o)? (How many?) is followed by a plural noun.

When the noun is not expressed "Faint?" is used.

e.g. Edrychwch, maen nhw'n gwerthu afalau.   **Look,** they sell apples.
     Faint rydych chi eisiau?   How many do you want?

"Faint (o)?" also means "How much?" and when used in this sense is followed by a singular noun as in English.

e.g. Faint o amser sy gyda chi?   How much time have you got?
     Faint sy gyda chi?   How much have you got?

Note also the idiomatic use of "Faint o" in the question "Faint o'r gloch ydy hi?" (What time is it?).

(b) "Sawl (How many?) is followed by a singular noun.

e.g. Sawl ceiniog sy ar y bwrdd?   How many pennies are there on the table?

"Sawl un?" is used when the noun is not expressed.

e.g. Sawl un sy gyda chi?   How many have you got?

(c) "Pa?" (Which?), "Sut?" (What kind of?) cause soft mutation to the noun.

Pa dudalen rydych chi'n ddarllen?   What page are you reading?
Sut dŷ sy gyda chi?   What kind of a house have you got?

6 When a question ends in a preposition in English, that preposition comes at the beginning of the question in Welsh.

e.g. *O* ble mae'r bachgen yn dod?   Where does the boy come *from*?
     I ble maen nhw'n mynd?   Where are they going *to*?

RESPONSE TO STATEMENTS

A response can be made to a statement in the same way as to a question.

e.g. *Question*
     Ydy John yn y tŷ?   Is John in the house?
     Ydy.   Yes.
     Nag ydy.   No.

Statement

Mae John yn y tŷ.	John is in the house.
Ydy.	Yes.
Nag ydy.	No.

Similarly:

Mae llyfr ar y bwrdd.	There's a book on the		Roedd hi'n dost.	She was ill.
Oes.	Yes.	(table.	Oedd.	Yes.
Nag oes.	No.		Nag oedd.	No.
Daethoch chi ar y bws.	You came on the bus.		Yn yr ysgol mae e.	He is in school.
Do.	Yes.		Ie.	Yes.
Naddo.	No.		Nage.	No.

OND

1 "Ond" (= onid) is sometimes used in a sentence to convey astonishment or amazement. It can be used:

(*a*) to introduce a sentence
e.g. Ond ydy hi'n braf?   Isn't it fine?

(*b*) as a tag at the end of a sentence
e.g. Mae hi'n braf, ond ydy hi?   It's fine, isn't it?

The intonation of the voice expresses this astonishment or amazement.

2 "Ond" can also be used as a tag without any emphasis or expression of astonishment, merely to turn a statement into a question as in the English "It's raining, isn't it?"
e.g. Mae hi'n bwrw glaw, ond ydy hi?

Further examples

Rydych chi'n mynd, ond ydych chi?	You're going, aren't you?
Mae e'n rhedeg, ond ydy e?	He's running, isn't he?
Roedd hi yna, ond oedd hi?	She was there, wasn't she?
Byddan nhw'n canu, ond byddan nhw?	They'll be singing, won't they?
Basech chi'n hoffi dod, ond basech chi?	You would like to come, wouldn't you
Aeth e i weld y gêm, ond do?	He went to the game, didn't he?
Es i i Gaerdydd ddoe, ond do?	I went to Cardiff yesterday, didn't I?

Note the use of "ond do" in the Past Tense.

In South Wales the tendancy is to add "fe" after "do", irrespective of the person.

e.g. Cyrhaeddodd e'n gynnar, ond do fe?	He arrived early, didn't he?
Prynon nhw ddillad newydd, ond do fe?	They bought new clothes, didn't they?

Similarly "e" is often used in South Wales after oes, oedd and bydd.

e.g. Mae llawer o bobl yma, ond oes e?	There are a lot of people here, aren't there?
Roedd pen tost gyda fi, ond oedd e?	I had a head-ache, didn't I?
Bydd peth ar ôl, ond bydd e?	There will be some left, won't there?

"Yna" pronounced "'na" is used in North Wales instead of "e".

e.g. Roedd pen tost gyda fi, ond oedd yna?

Bydd peth ar ôl, ond bydd yna?

Note

1 An affirmative statement is generally followed by a negative tag.

e.g. Mae e'n byw yng Nghaerffili ond ydy e?　　He lives in Caerffili, doesn't he?

2 A negative statement is generally followed by an affirmative tag.

e.g. Dydy chi ddim yn byw yn Abertawe, ydych chi?　　You don't live in Swansea, do you?

Note that "ond" does not form part of the tag following a negative statement.

MISCELLANEOUS

Y naill . . . y llall (the one . . . the other)

e.g. Roedd y naill yn wyn a'r llall yn las.　　The one was white and the other was blue.

Note the plural form **y naill . . .y lleill**

With adjectives or demonstrative elements **yr un . . . y llall (the one . . . the other)** is used.

e.g. Cymerais i'r un melyn a cymerodd hi'r llall.　　I took the yellow one and she took the other.

Plural form: **y rhai . . . y lleill (the ones . . . the others)**

Y naill/yr un + noun . . . + noun + arall (the one + noun . . . + the other + noun)

e.g. Mae'r naill frawd/un brawd yn dal a'r brawd arall yn fyr.　　The one brother is tall and the other brother is short.

Note that "naill" causes soft mutation to the nouns that follow.

Un . . . arall (one . . . another)

e.g. Peidiwch rhoi mwy i un bachgen nag i fachgen arall.　　Don't give more to one boy than to another boy.

Plural form: **rhai . . . eraill (some . . . others)**

e.g. Roedd rhai yn gall ag eraill yn ffôl.　　Some were wise and others were foolish.

Un/rhyw + noun . . . noun + arall/eraill (One/some + noun . . . another/other + noun).

e.g. Os ydy hyn yn iawn i un dyn, mae e'n iawn i ddyn arall.　　If this is right for one man, it is right for another man.

Achos roedd rhyw blentyn wedi bod yn ddrwg yn y dosbarth, cafodd y plant eraill i gyd eu cosbi gyda fe.　　Because some child had been naughty in the class, all the other children were punished with him.

Note that "rhyw" causes soft mutation to the nouns that follow.

Naill ai . . . neu (either . . . or)

e.g. Rydyn ni naill ai'n mynd i Sbaen neu i Ffrainc.   We are either going to Spain or to France.

Un (one)

Mae un ci a tair cath gyda ni.   We've got one dog and three cats.

If "un" refers to one of several, then it is followed by "o".

e.g. Roedd un o'r plant yn dost.   One of the children was ill.

"Un" can also convey the meaning "the one and the same".

e.g. Rydw i'n byw yn yr un lle â fe.   I live in the same place as he.

"Yr un" is used to denote the English "each".

e.g. Cafodd y plant bunt yr un.   The children had a pound each.

Note the use of "un" in the following:

unwaith (once)   unrhyw (any)   unman/unlle (anywhere)

"Un" is used with "pa" to form the interrogative particle "P'un?" (which one?).

e.g. P'un ydy'r gorau?   Which one is the best?

Rhyw (a certain, some)

e.g. Mae rhyw ddyn wrth y drws.   There's some man at the door.

Roedd rhyw raglen o faes yr eisteddfod ar y teledu neithiwr.   There was a (certain) programme from the eisteddfod field on the television last night.

"Rhyw" can be used before a verb-noun to suggest that the action of the verb is indefinite.

e.g. Rhyw gysgu roeddwn i.   I was (sort of) sleeping.

Note that "rhyw" causes soft mutation.

"Rhyw" forms the first element in several compound words.

e.g.			
rhywbeth	something	rhywfath	some kind
rhywun	someone	rhywfodd ⎫	somehow
rhywrai	some people	rhywsut ⎭	
rhywle	some place	rhywffordd	some way
rhywdro ⎫	sometime		
rhywbryd ⎭			

Similarly "rhyw" can form the second element in certain words.

e.g. unrhyw   any

Peth (some, a little)

e.g. Mae peth arian gyda fi.	I've got some/a little money.
Roedd peth o'r gwaith yn dda.	Some of the work was good.

"Peth" is now used as an interrogative pronoun in its mutated form "Beth?" ("Pa beth?") What?

Note the use of "peth" in some idioms:

e.g. o dipyn i beth	gradually
peth amser	some time
truan o beth	a pityful thing

Llawer (many, much, a lot, several)

e.g. Oedd llawer yna neithiwr?　　Were there many there last night?

When a noun follows "llawer" it is preceded by "o".

e.g. Daeth llawer o bobl i'r cyngerdd.　　Many people came to the concert.

Note the use of "llawer" in the following phrases:

llawer gwaith	many times
llawer gwell	much better
llawer mwy	much more
llawer iawn	very many, a great deal
rhyw lawer	many (when the number referred to is indefinite or a relatively small number)

Ychydig (a small number (a) few, (a) little)

Dim ond ychydig o'r plant oedd yn yr ysgol ddoe.	Only a few of the children were in school yesterday.
Faint oedd yna? Ychydig.	How many were there? A few.

Digon (enough, sufficient, plenty)

Roedd digon o fwyd yn y parti.	There was enough food in the party.
Oes arian gyda chi? Oes, digon.	Have you got any money? Yes, plenty.

Gormod (too much, too many)

Roedd gormod o annwyd arni hi.	She had too much of a cold.
Rydych chi wedi gwahodd gormod.	You have invited too many.

Rhagor (more)

Ydych chi eisiau rhagor o de?	Do you want more tea?
Gobeithio daw rhagor.	I hope that more will come.

Llawn (full)

Roedd y tŷ'n llawn o fwg.	The house was full of smoke.
Ydy'r dosbarth yn llawn?	Is the class full?

Cymaint (so much, so many)

Daeth cymaint o bobl i weld y briodas.	So many people came to see the wedding.
Roedd cymaint yn y neuadd.	There was so much in the hall.

Tamaid (a bit)

Dyma damaid o gaws i chi.	Here's a bit of cheese for you.
Mae tamaid ar y plât.	There's a bit on the plate.

Dim byd (anything, nothing)

This is used in negative sentences only.

e.g. Doedd dim byd yna.	There wasn't anything there.
Beth sy'n bod? Dim byd.	What's the matter? Nothing.

Dim (none, any)

Does dim bara yn y tŷ.	There isn't any bread in the house.
Oedd arian gyda chi? Nag oedd. Dim.	Did you have any money? No. None.

"Dim/ddim" is also used to indicate the negative form of the verb.

e.g. Ddaw e ddim.	He won't come.
Does dim llyfr gyda fi.	I haven't got a book.

Neb (anyone, no one)

This is chiefly used in negative sentences.

e.g. Welais i neb.	I didn't see anyone.
Pwy oedd yna? Neb.	Who was there? No one.

Pawb (everyone), Pob (every, each)

"Pawb" is used as a pronoun and is regarded as a singular form. But when a personal pronoun is used in place of it, it is regarded as plural.

e.g. Ydy pawb yma? Ydyn.	Is everyone here? Yes (they are).

"Pob" is used as an adjective and is followed by a noun or pronominal.

e.g. pob merch	every/each girl
pob un	every/each one

"Pob" forms the first element in several compound words.

e.g. popeth	everything
pobman	everywhere

Note the use of "pob" in the following idioms:

bob yn un, bob yn un ag un	one by one
bob yn ddau, bob yn ddau a dau	two by two
bob yn ail	alternatively
bob yn eilddydd	every other day
bob yn dipyn	bit by bit

"Bob" is often used in adverbial phrases.

e.g. bob dydd   every day
      bob nos   every night
      bob blwyddyn   every year

Cwbl (all, everything, complete/ly, entire/ly)

Dyna'r cwbl.   That is all.
Ydy'r cwbl yma?   Is everything here?
Roedd hi'n gwbl ddall.   She was completely blind.

Note the following phrase:

dim o gwbl   not at all

Y Fath/Sut = Such

Such can be used (a) with nouns and (b) with nouns described by adjectives.
"Y fath"/"sut" is placed before the noun.

    e.g. (a)Mae'r fath bobl yn brin. ⎫
       Mae sut bobl yn brin.   ⎬ Such people are rare.

      (b) Rydyn ni'n cael y fath dywydd da. ⎱ We're having such fine weather.
         Rydyn ni'n cael sut dywydd da.   ⎰

Note that the noun following "y fath"/"sut" undergoes soft mutation.

Note also that "mor" conveys the meaning "such" and it precedes the adjective which describes the noun.

    e.g. Mae'r plant yn aros yn y tŷ achos rydyn   The children are staying in the house
       ni'n cael tywydd mor wael.   because we're having such poor weather.

Note that the adjective following "mor" undergoes soft mutation (except "ll" and "rh").

I'w + Verb-Noun

This conveys the equivalent of the Passive Infinitive in English.

    e.g. 1 Dyma rywbeth i'w fwyta.   Here's something to eat (= to be eaten).

       2 Dyma ferch i'w phriodi.   Here's a girl to marry (= to be married to).

       3 Dyma lyfrau i'w darllen.   Here are some books to read (= to be read).

Note that the mutations following "i'w" depend on the gender and number of the preceding nouns:

Soft mutation after a masculine noun (Example 1).

Aspirate mutation (of p, t, c) after a feminine noun (Example 2).

No mutation after a plural noun (Example 3).

In speech, however, the tendency is to ignore these differences and apply soft mutation to them all and the " 'w" in the form "i'w" disappears.

    e.g. Dyma rywbeth i fwyta.   Dyma ferch i briodi.   Dyma lyfrau i ddarllen.

But when the "i'w" expresses the equivalent of the pronoun object in English, then it is retained.

    e.g. Rydw i'n mynd i'w weld e.   I'm going to see him.
         Rydw i'n mynd i'w gweld hi.   I'm going to see her.
         Rydw i'n mynd i'w gweld nhw.   I'm going to see them.

Ar + Verb-Noun conveys the meaning "about", "on the point of".

    e.g. Roeddwn i ar fynd pan ddaeth John.   I was about to go when John came.

Note that "ar" causes soft mutation to the verb-noun.

"Ar fin" without a mutation can also be used to express the same meaning.

    e.g. Roeddwn i ar fin mynd pan ddaeth   I was about to go when John came.
         John.

PRICES
Typical Questions

Faint ydy pris . . .?	What is the price of . . .? How much is . . .?

    e.g. Faint ydy pris yr wyau?   What is the price of the eggs?

Faint ydy e/hi?   How much is it?
Faint ydyn nhw?   How much are they?

Model Answers

    (a) Ceiniog, dwy ceiniog, tair ceiniog, etc.   A penny, two pence, three pence, etc.

    (b) Hanner can ceiniog y pwys.   Fifty pence a pound.
       ,,   ,,   ,, y kilogram.   ,,   ,, a kilogram.
       ,,   ,,   ,, y galwyn.   ,,   ,, a gallon.
       ,,   ,,   ,, y litr, etc.   ,,   ,, a litre, etc.

(In this context "a pound" etc. is expressed in Welsh by placing the article "y/yr" in front of "pwys" etc.)

    (c) Punt yr un.   A pound each.

(Note that "yr un" is used to denote the English "each").

Yn/mewn = In

    (a) The noun that follows "yn" is definite.

    e.g. Yn y tŷ.   In the house.

    (b) The noun that follows "mewn" is indefinite.

    e.g. mewn tŷ   in a house

Wrth

Note the idiomatic usage of "wrth" in the following phrases.

(a) wrth y galwyn   by the gallon   wrth y llathen   by the yard
     wrth y litr   by the litre   wrth y metr   by the metre

(b) wrth ei olwg e   according to his appearance

The verb "barnu" (to judge) is followed by "wrth" in this context.

e.g. Rydw i'n barnu wrth ei olwg e.   I'm judging according to (by) his appearance.

Note the following questions and answers. (These are often used in speech)

(a) Wnewch chi?   Will you?
     Gwna.   Yes (I will).
     Na wna.   No (I will not).

(b) Ga i . . .?   May I?/May I have . . .?
     Cewch.   Yes (you may/may have . . .)
     Na chewch.   No (you may not/may not have . . .).

e.g. Wnewch chi ddod?   Will you come?
     Gwna/Na wna.   Yes/No.
     Ga i gwpanaid o de?   May I have a cup of tea?
     Cewch/Na chewch.   Yes/No.

Note that the object takes soft mutation in these examples.

A few nouns vary in their gender, being regarded as masculine nouns in some areas and as feminine nouns in others.

e.g. munud (minute)   cornel (corner)
      dwy funud (f.) ⎫two minutes   y cornel (m.) ⎫the corner
      dau funud (m.) ⎭   y gornel (f.) ⎭

Scarcely, hardly

The simplest way to express this meaning is as follows:

Dydyn nhw braidd yn gweld ei gilydd.   They scarcely see one another.

Note that the verb is negative although the negative "ddim" is not used.

Note: "Braidd" is also used to express the meaning "rather".

Mae'r tywydd braidd yn oer.   The weather is rather cold.

Almost

The simplest way to express this meaning is as follows:

Mae'r botel bron yn llawn.   The bottle is almost full.
Rydw i bron yn gallu deall.   I can almost understand.

TIME

Note that in Welsh the feminine pronoun is used when referring to the time.

e.g. Faint o'r gloch ydy hi?   What time is it?
      Mae hi'n un o'r gloch.   It's one o' clock.

Note also the use of "'n"(the abbreviated form of "yn") which causes soft mutation. Hence:

Mae hi'n *d*ri o'r gloch.	It's three o'clock.
Mae hi'n *b*ump o'r gloch.	It's five o'clock.
Mae hi'n *dd*eg o'r gloch.	Its' ten o'clock.

When referring to time, the traditional numbers "un ar ddeg, deuddeg" etc. are still used rather than "un deg un, un deg dau" etc.

e.g. Mae hi'n un ar ddeg o'r gloch.	It's eleven o'clock.
Mae hi'n ddeuddeg o'r gloch.	It's twelve o'clock.

Note the following constructions:

(*a*) Mae hi'n bum munud wedi dau.	It's five (minutes) past two.
Mae hi'n ddeg munud wedi un.	It's ten (minutes) past one.
Mae hi'n chwarter wedi tri.	It's a quarter past three.
Mae hi'n ugain munud wedi pedwar.	It's twenty (minutes) past four.
Mae hi'n bum munud ar hugain wedi pump.	It's twenty five (minutes) past five.
Mae hi'n hanner awr wedi deg.	It's half past ten.

Note that there is no mutation after the preposition "wedi".

(*b*) Mae hi'n bum munud i *dd*au.	It's five (minutes) to two.
Mae hi'n ddeg munud i *d*ri.	It's ten (minutes) to three.
Mae hi'n chwarter i *b*edwar.	It's a quarter to four.
Mae hi'n ugain munud i *dd*eg.	It's twenty (minutes) to ten.
Mae hi'n bum munud ar hugain i *dd*euddeg.	It's twenty five (minutes) to twelve.

Note that the preposition "i" causes soft mutation.

Note the following phrases:

am ddau o'r gloch.	at two o'clock

(Note the soft mutation after the preposition "am".)

erbyn pump o'r gloch.	by five o'clock
bron yn ddeg o'r gloch	nearly ten o'clock.

"Newydd" before the verb-noun conveys the meaning "just".

e.g. Mae hi newydd droi tri o'r gloch.	It has just turned three o'clock.
Maen nhw newydd fynd.	They have just gone.

Note the use of the interrogative "Pryd?" (At what time? When?).

e.g. Pryd rydych chi'n codi yn y bore?	At what time/When do you get up in the morning?

This should not be confused with the conjunction "pan" = when.

i.e. Pryd cyrhaeddon nhw? When did they arrive?

Pan gyrhaeddon nhw, cawson nhw groeso cynnes. When they arrived, they had a warm welcome.

LETTER WRITING

Setting out a letter

(*a*) Informal (to a friend or acquaintance).

> 7 Ffordd yr Ysgol,
> Aberafon,
> Caerfyrddin.
>
> Ionawr 15, 1998

Annwyl (Mair, Mr. Huws, etc.)

. . . .

. . . .

. . . .

> Cofion cynnes (Warm regards)
> Cofion caredig (Kind regards)
> Dymuniadau gorau (Best wishes)
> Pob hwyl (All the best)

(*b*) Formal

> Sŵn y Môr,
> Llanfair,
> Caernarfon,
> Gwynedd.
>
> Mehefin 23, 1998

Y Llyfrgellydd,
Llyfrgell y Dref,
Caernarfon,
Gwynedd.

Annwyl (Syr, Mr. Jones, etc.)

. . . .

. . . .

. . . .

> Yr eiddoch yn gywir (Yours sincerely)

TABLE OF MUTATIONS

Initial Consonant	Soft	Nasal	Aspirate
P pensil (pencil)	B ei bensil e (his pencil)	MH fy mhensil i (my pencil)	PH ei phensil hi (her pencil)
T tad (father)	D ei dad e (his father)	NH fy nhad i (my father)	TH ei thad hi (her father)
C ci (dog)	G ei gi e (his dog)	NGH fy nghi i (my dog)	CH ei chi hi (her dog)
B brawd (brother)	F ei frawd e (his brother)	M fy mrawd i (my brother)	NO CHANGE
D dosbarth (class)	DD ei ddosbarth e (his class)	N fy nosbarth i (my class)	NO CHANGE
G gardd (garden)	— ei ardd e (his garden)	NG fy ngardd i (my garden)	NO CHANGE
LL llyfr (book)	L ei lyfr e (his book)	NO CHANGE	NO CHANGE
M mam (mother)	F ei fam e (his mother)	NO CHANGE	NO CHANGE
RH rhaglen (programme)	R ei raglen e (his programme)	NO CHANGE	NO CHANGE

SOFT MUTATION

Nouns

1 Feminine singular nouns after the article "y", except for nouns beginning with "ll" and "rh".

    e.g. y ferch   the girl
          y ddesg   the desk
          y llwy   the spoon

2 Nouns after the adjectives.

    e.g. hen ddyn   an old man
          unig fab   an only son
          rhyw ddydd   some day

This also applies when an adjective forms part of a noun phrase and comes in front of a noun.

    e.g. prifweinidog   prime minister

There are some exceptions. There is no mutation after the comparative and equative forms.

    e.g. cystal dydd   such a good day
          gwell dydd   a better day

Similarly when "rhai", "peth", "sawl" and "pob" are used as adjectives there is no mutation in the nouns that follow.

    e.g. rhai plant   some children
          peth bwyd   some food
          sawl gwaith   several times
          pob dydd   every day

3 After the personal pronouns "dy", "ei", (m.), "'i" (m.), "'w" (m.).

    e.g. dy dad di   your father
          ei frawd e   his brother
          o'i dŷ e   from his house
          i'w deulu e   to his family

4 After the prepositions "am, ar, at, dan, dros, drwy, heb, i, o, wrth, gan, hyd".

    e.g. am bunt   for a pound
          ar gadair   on a chair
          i Gaerfyrddin   to Carmarthen

5 After the numerals "un" with feminine nouns (except those beginning with "ll" and "rh"), "dau" and "dwy".

e.g. un gath   one cat
     dau gi   two dogs
     dwy dref   two towns
     un llaw   one hand
     un rhaw   one spade

6 "Dau" and "dwy" after "y".

e.g. y ddau (fachgen)   the two (boys)
     y ddwy (ferch)   the two (girls)

7 Ordinal numbers, when they are feminine after the article "y".

e.g. y bumed (ferch)   the fifth (girl)
     y ddegfed (wers)   the tenth (lesson)

Note also that feminine singular nouns mutate after these ordinals.

8 Nouns after the predicative "yn", except for nouns beginning with "ll" and "rh".

e.g. Rydw i'n ddyn tal.   I am a tall man.

But note:
    Mae e'n llenor da.   He is a good literary man.

9 The direct object of an inflected verb.

e.g. Gwelais i gar o flaen y tŷ neithiwr.   I saw a car in front of the house last night.

10 After the conjunction "neu".

e.g. mab neu ferch.   a son or a daughter.

This includes verb-nouns (e.g. ennill neu golli—win or lose) but not the inflected form of the verb (e.g. Gwrandewch ar y radio neu byddwch yn dawel—Listen to the radio or be quiet).

11 After "dyma", "dyna" and "dacw".

e.g. Dyma gi da.   Here's a good dog.
     Dyna gartref Gwilym.   There's Gwilym's home.
     Dacw dŷ Aled.   There's Aled's house (over there).

12 Nouns in the vocative case.

e.g. Ferched! Dewch yma!   Girls! Come here!
     Bore da blant!   Good morning children!

13 After an intervening word i.e. a break in the normal order of words.

    e.g. Mae yn y farchnad ddigon o ddewis.   There is in the market plenty of choice.

This type of sentence is more common in literary Welsh. However, "yna" is frequently interposed in speech after the third person singular of the verb "bod" (to be). It does not convey any meaning and must be followed by an indefinite subject.

    e.g. Mae yna dŷ newydd yn y pentref.   There's a new house in the village.

Adjectives

1 After a feminine singular noun.

    e.g. mam dda   a good mother
         merch dal   a tall girl

2 In comparison of adjectives after "mor" and "cyn" in the equative and after "yn" in the comparative except for adjectives beginning with "ll" and "rh".

    e.g. Mae Rhys mor dal â Gareth.   Rhys is as tall as Gareth.
         Roedd e cyn daled â'i frawd.   He was as tall as his brother.
         Mae e'n fwy na chi.   He is bigger than you.
         Rhedais i cyn gynted â mellten.   I ran as fast as lightning.
         Dydy siopau Caerdydd ddim mor rhad â   Cardiff shops are not as cheap as
           siopau Caerfyrddin.   Carmarthen shops.
         Ydy Huw yn llai na'i frawd?   Is Huw smaller than his brother?

3 After the adverbs "rhy", "lled", "gweddol", "go", and "mor". However, after "mor" no mutation occurs to adjectives beginning with "ll" and "rh".

    e.g. rhy fach   too small
         lled dda   quite good/fairly well
         gweddol lonydd   fairly still/calm
         go wlyb   quite/fairly wet
         mor rhwydd   so easy

4 After "yn" except for words beginning with "ll" and "rh".

    e.g. Mae'r llyfr yn dda.   The book is good.
         Mae'r plant yn ddrwg.   The children are naughty.

5 When an adjective comes in front of a noun, as part of the direct object noun phrase, not only does it cause soft mutation, but it undergoes soft mutation itself, exactly as the noun does. Two common examples are "cyn" (former) and "prif" (chief).

    e.g. Es i i brifddinas Lloegr ddoe.   I went to the capital city of England
                                         yesterday.

         Dyma gyn brifathrawes Siân.   Here is Sian's former headmistress.
         Mae e'n brifweinidog gwael.   He is a poor prime minister.

Similarly when the adjectives "rhai" and "peth" are used as part of the noun phrase, they come in front of the noun, and undergo soft mutation.

e.g. Dyna beth llaeth. There's some milk.
Prynais i rai llyfrau. I bought some books.

But note that there is no mutation to the nouns that follow these adjectives.

6 After the conjunction "neu".

e.g. du neu frown black or brown
mawr neu fach big or small

Verbs

1 Interrogative forms of the inflected verb.

e.g. Fuoch chi'n nofio? Have you been swimming?/Did you swim?
Weloch chi'ch ffrindiau? Did you see your friends?

(In literary Welsh, the interrogative particle "a" precedes these forms and causes a mutation. The particle "a" has now disappeared from the spoken language but the mutation remains.)

2 Negative forms of the inflected verb beginning with b, d, g, ll, m, rh (verbs beginning with p, t, and c undergo aspirate mutation).

e.g. Welais i ddim byd. I didn't see anything.
Ddarllenais i ddim o'r llyfr. I didn't read the book.

(In literary Welsh, the negative particle "ni" precedes these forms and causes soft mutation with verbs beginning with b, d, g, ll, m, rh. This particle is no longer heard in the spoken language but the mutation it causes still remains.)

3 After the particles "fe" and "mi".

e.g. Fe/Mi glywais i. I heard.
Fe/Mi redodd e. He ran.

4 After the relative pronoun "a" and the negative relative pronoun "na". "Na" causes soft mutation with verbs beginning with b, g, d, ll, m and rh. However, verbs beginning with p, t and c undergo aspirate mutation after "na".

e.g. Dyma'r dyn (a) ddaeth i'r ysgol. This is/Here is the man who came to school.

(This relative pronoun is often left out in spoken Welsh but the mutation it causes remains.)

Dyma'r dyn na ddaeth i'r ysgol.

> This is/Here is the man who didn't come to school.

Note an alternative negative form often used in conversation. (See page 78).

Dyma'r dyn ddaeth ddim i'r ysgol.

5 After "a" (whether)

e.g. Fe ofynnodd e i fi (a) faswn i'n mynd.

> He asked me whether I would be going.

(This particle is often omitted in speech but the mutation it causes remains).

6 After the conjunction "pan".
e.g. Pan ddes i . . .

> When I came . . .

7 After the interrogative pronouns "Beth" and "Pwy". (See page 102).

e.g. Beth wnaethoch chi?   What did you do?
Pwy welodd e?   Whom did he see?

Adverbial Phrases

Nouns and adjectives forming part of an adverbial phrase sometimes mutate.

e.g. Gwelais i John ddydd Sadwrn diwetha.   I saw John last Saturday.
This rule is no longer rigidly observed, but note that the mutation is always found in certain phrases.

e.g. bob amser   always
bob dydd   every day
bob tro   everytime
ddoe   yesterday

ASPIRATE MUTATION

1 After the personal pronouns "ei", "'i" (b) and "'w" (b).

e.g. ei thad hi   her father
o'i chartref hi   from her home
i'w thŷ hi   to her house

2 After the prepositions "â", "gyda", "tua".

e.g. Es i â chi drws nesa am dro.   I took the dog next door for a walk.
gyda chyllell a fforc   with a knife and fork
tua phump o'r gloch.   about five o'clock

This rule does not apply in many dialects.

e.g. gyda cannwyll   with a candle

3 After the conjunction "a".

    e.g. cath a chi   a cat and dog

    This rule does not apply in many dialects.

    e.g. dau a tri.   two and three.

    However, it remains in well established phrases.

    e.g. papur a phensil   paper and pencil

4 Negative forms of the inflected verb.

        Ches i ddim byd.   I didn't have anything.
        Phrynais i ddim o'r losin.   I didn't buy the sweets.
        Thalais i ddim.   I didn't pay.

(In literary Welsh the negative particle "ni" precedes these forms and causes aspirate mutation with verbs beginning with p, t, c. This particle is no longer heard in the spoken language but the mutation it causes still remains.)

5 Comparison of adjectives—after "â" in the equative and "na" in the comparative.

    e.g. Mae'r bachgen cyn gryfed â chawr.   The boy is as strong as a giant.
         Mae ci Alun yn fwy na chi Gwilym.   Alun's dog is bigger than Gwilym's dog.

    (These rules do not apply in many dialects.)

6 After the negative form of the relative pronoun "na" (with p, t, c).

    e.g. Dyma'r dyn na thalodd am ei ginio.   Here is/This is the man who didn't pay for his dinner.

    Note the alternative form used in conversation.

    e.g. Dyma'r dyn thalodd ddim am ei ginio.

7 After "tra".

    e.g. tra chyfoethog   very/exceedingly rich
    This usage is mainly found in literary Welsh.

NASAL MUTATION

1 After the personal pronoun "fy".
    e.g. fy nhŷ i   my house

2 After the preposition "yn".

    e.g. yng Nghaernarfon   in Caernarfon

3 "Blynedd" (the form used instead of "blwyddyn" with numerals) and "blwydd" (the form used instead of "blwyddyn" to tell one's age) after pum, saith, wyth, naw, deg/deng" and any numeral incorporating the forms "deg" and "ugain".

e.g. pymtheg (mlwydd) oed   fifteen years old
     deuddeg (mlwydd) oed   twelve years old
     un deg saith mlynedd   seventeen years
     naw mlynedd   nine years

This rule formerly applied to "diwrnod" (day), but it has by now largely disappeared.

SELECTED VOCABULARY AND IDIOMS

Dyddiau'r wythnos

The following are all masculine:

Dydd Sul	*Sunday*
Dydd Llun	*Monday*
Dydd Mawrth	*Tuesday*
Dydd Mercher	*Wednesday*
Dydd Iau	*Thursday*
Dydd Gwener	*Friday*
Dydd Sadwrn	*Saturday*

Misoedd y Flwyddyn

(Mis)	Ionawr	*January*
,,	Chwefror	*February*
,,	Mawrth	*March*
,,	Ebrill	*April*
,,	Mai	*May*
,,	Mehefin	*June*
,,	Gorffennaf	*July*
,,	Awst	*August*
,,	Medi	*September*
,,	Hydref	*October*
,,	Tachwedd	*November*
,,	Rhagfyr	*December*

Y Tymhorau

Y Gwanwyn	*Spring*
Yr Haf	*Summer*
Yr Hydref	*Autumn*
Y Gaeaf	*Winter*

(Note the use of the article "y/yr" before the names of seasons.)

Enwau Gwledydd

Affrica *Africa*
Awstralia *Australia*
Awstria *Austria*
Cymru *Wales*
Ewrop *Europe*
Ffrainc *France*
Groeg *Greece*
Gwlad Belg *Belgium*
Iwerddon *Ireland*
Lloegr *England*
Llydaw *Brittany*
Norwy *Norway*
Sbaen *Spain*
Seland Newydd *New Zealand*
Twrci *Turkey*
Yr Aifft *Egypt*
Yr Alban *Scotland*
Yr Almaen *Germany*
Yr Eidal *Italy*
Yr India *India*
Yr Iseldiroedd *Holland*
Y Swistir *Switzerland*
Yr Unol Daleithiau *United States*

Enwau Dinasoedd a Threfi

Aberdaugleddau *Milford Haven*
Abergwaun *Fishguard*
Aberhonddu *Brecon*
Abertawe *Swansea*
Aberteifi *Cardigan*
Amwythig *Shrewsbury*
Bryste *Bristol*
Caerdydd *Cardiff*
Caerfyrddin *Carmarthen*
Caergybi *Holyhead*
Caernarfon *Caernarvon*
Casnewydd *Newport*
Castell-nedd *Neath*
Dinbych *Denbigh*
Lerpwl *Liverpool*
Llundain *London*
Manceinion *Manchester*
Tyddewi *St. David's*
Wrecsam *Wrexham*
Y Barri *Barry*
Y Drenewydd *Newtown*
Yr Wyddgrug *Mold*
Y Trallwng *Welshpool*

Gorchmynion

Agorwch y drws — *Open the door*
Allan o'r ffordd — *Out of the way*
Arhoswch funud — *Wait a minute*
Byddwch yn ofalus — *Be careful*
Caewch y drws — *Close the door*
Daliwch ati — *Keep at it*
Dewch i chwarae — *Come to play*
Dewch i ddawnsio — *Come and dance*
Dewch i mewn — *Come inside*
Dewch yma — *Come here*
Dewch ymlaen — *Come along*
Edrychwch yma — *Look here*
Ewch adre — *Go home*
Ewch allan — *Go outside*
Ewch i ffwrdd — *Go away*
Ewch i mewn — *Go inside*
Ewch i nôl — *Fetch*
Ewch ymlaen — *Go on, go along*

Gorchmynion

Ewch i ymolchi	*Go to wash*
Ewch yn ôl	*Go back*
Gadewch i ni fynd	*Let's go*
Gwrandewch arna i	*Listen to me*
I ffwrdd â chi	*Away with you*
Peidiwch (â) siarad dwli	*Don't talk nonsense*
Peidiwch (ag) anghofio	*Don't forget*
Sefwch yn llonydd	*Stand still*
Trowch drosodd	*Turn over*
Trowch y tudalen	*Turn the page*

Cyfarchion

Beth sy'n bod?	*What is the matter?*
Beth ydy'ch enw chi?	*What is you name?*
Bore da	*Good morning*
Da boch chi	*Farewell, goodbye*
Da iawn, diolch	*Very well, thank you*
Diolch	*Thank you*
Diolch yn fawr	*Thank you very much*
Dyma gwpanaid o de i chi	*Here is a cup of tea for you*
Faint o'r gloch ydy hi?	*What is the time?*
Nos da	*Good night*
Pob lwc	*The best of luck*
Prynhawn da	*Good afternoon*
Sut rydych chi?	*How are you?*

Cymariaethau

Cyhyd â blwyddyn	*As long as a year*
Cyn ddistawed â'r bedd	*As quiet as the grave*
Mor ddistaw â'r bedd	
Cyn falched â'r paun	*As proud as a peacock*
Mor falch â'r paun	
Cyn gynted â mellten	*As quick as lightning*
Mor gyflym â mellten	
Cyn lased â'r môr	*As blue as the sea*
Mor las â'r môr	
Cyn wired â'r pader	*As true as the Lord's Prayer*
Mor wir â'r pader	
Mor araf â malwoden	*As slow as a snail*
Mor dew â mochyn	*As fat as a pig*
Mor dlawd â llygoden eglwys	*As poor as a church mouse*

Mor drwm â plwm	*As heavy as lead*
Mor dywyll â'r fagddu	*Pitch dark*
Mor ddiniwed â'r oen	*As innocent as a lamb*
Mor ddistaw â llygoden	*As quiet as a mouse*
Mor ddu â bol buwch	*As dark as a cow's stomach*
Mor ddu â'r glo/â'r frân	*As black as coal/the crow*
Mor felys â siwgr	*As sweet as sugar*
Mor gryf â ceffyl	*As strong as a horse*
Mor iach â'r gneuen	*As fit as a fiddle (nut)*
Mor lân â'r aur	*As pure as gold*
Mor llawen â'r gog	*As happy as the lark (cuckoo)*
Mor llithrig â'r rhew	*As slippery as ice*
Mor olau â'r haul	*As bright as the sun*
Mor sâl â ci	*As sick as a dog*
Mor sobr â sant	*As sober as a judge (saint)*
Mor syth â ffon	*As straight as a line (stick)*
Mor wan â blewyn	*As weak as a kitten (hair)*
Mor ystyfnig â mul	*As stubborn as a mule*
Yn boeth fel tân	*As hot as a fire*
Yn canu fel aderyn	*Singing like a bird*
Yn crio fel babi	*Crying like a baby*
Yn crynu fel deilen	*Shaking like a leaf*
Yn dlws fel darlun	*Pretty as a picture*
Yn goch fel gwaed	*Red like blood*
Yn grwn fel afal	*Round as an apple*
Yn gwaedu fel mochyn	*Bleeding like a pig*
Yn gweld fel cath	*Eyes like a cat*
Yn gyflym fel y gwynt	*Fast as the wind*
Yn gyfrwys fel llwynog	*Sly as a fox*
Yn rhuo fel llew	*Roaring like a lion*
Ymhellach na	*Further than*
Yn ysgafn fel pluen	*Light as a feather*

Idiomau

Â'i ben yn ei blu	*Dejected, sulking*
Â'i wynt yn ei ddwrn	*Out of breath*
Ar agor	*Open*
Ar bigau'r drain	*On tenterhooks*
Ar bob cyfrif	*On every account. By all means*
Ar ei ben ei hun(an)	*Alone*
Ar hyn o bryd	*Now. At the present time*
Ar doriad gwawr	*At dawn*
Arian drwg	*Forged money*
Ar y dechrau	*At first. At the beginning*

Idiomau

Beth am . . .?	*What about . . .?*
Beth bynnag	*However. Whatsoever*
Bob amser	*Always*
Bob cam	*All the way*
Bob yn ail	*Alternately*
Bob yn un	*One by one*
Bron (â) llwgu	*Almost famished*
Bwrw'r Sul	*To spend a weekend*
Byth a beunydd	*Forever and again*
Byth eto	*Never again*
Cael dau ben llinyn ynghyd	*To make ends meet*
Cael hwyl	*To have fun*
Canu'r delyn/piano	*To play the harp/piano*
Canu'n iach	*To bid farewell*
Cerdded ling-di-long	*To loiter*
Cerdded yn wysg ei gefn	*To walk backwards*
Codi ar ei draed	*To get to his feet*
Codi ar ei eistedd	*To sit up*
Cyn bo hir	*Before long*
Chwerthin am ben	*To laugh at*
Dan ganu	*Singing*
Deg ceiniog y pwys	*10p a pound*
Deg y cant	*Ten per cent (10%)*
Dillad isa	*Underclothes*
Diolch am hynny	*Thanks for that. Thank goodness*
Does dim rhyfedd	*No wonder*
Ddim eto	*Not again. Not yet*
Ddim i fod	*Not to be*
Erbyn hyn	*By now*
Er gwaetha	*Despite. In spite of*
Ei hun(an)	*Himself*
Ers meityn	*Since a long time*
Ers tro	*For some time*
Fin nos	*Evening*
Gorau po gynta	*The sooner the better*
Gadael y gath o'r cwd	*To let the cat out of the bag*
Gwneud fy ngorau glas	*Do my level best*
Hanner dydd	*Noon. Mid-day*
Hanner nos	*Mid-night*
Heb siw na miw	*Without a word or sound*
Hwnt ag yma	*Here and there*
Hyd yn oed	*Even*
Igam-ogam	*Zig-zag*
Llaesu dwylo	*To flag. To grow weary*

Lled cae	The width of a field
Lladd gwair	To cut hay/grass. To mow
Mae'n amlwg	It's obvious
Mae'n arllwys y glaw	It's pouring with rain
Mae ar ben arna i	It's all up with me. I'm finished
Mae'n braf	It's fine
Mae'n debyg	It seems
Mae eisiau bwyd arna i	I am in need of food
Mae'n draed moch arna i	I'm in a mess
Mae'n dda gen i/gyda fi	I'm glad/pleased
Mae'n ddrwg gen i/gyda fi	I'm sorry/I regret
Mae hiraeth arna i	I long for
Mae'n gyfleus	It's convenient
Mae'n hwyr	It's late
Mae'n gynnar	It's early
Mewn pryd	In time
Nerth ei ben	As loud as he could
Nerth ei draed	As fast as his legs could carry him
Newydd sbon	Brand new
O ben bwy'i gilydd	From end to end
O bryd i'w gilydd	From time to time
O chwith	The wrong way round
O ddrwg i waeth	From bad to worse
O gam i gam	Step by step
O'i gorun i'w sawdl	From head to foot
O'r diwedd	At last
O'r gorau	All right. Very well
O hyd	All the time. Continuously
Rhag blaen	Forthwith. At once
Rhag ofn	For fear. Lest
Rhoi'r ffidil yn y to	To give up
Rhywbryd eto	Sometime again
Sefyll arholiad	To sit an examination
Talu'n hallt	To pay dearly
Tipyn bach	A little
Trwy gydol y nos (Drwy . . .)	All through the night
Tu chwith	Inside out
Tybed	I wonder
Weithiau	Sometimes
Wrth ei bwysau	At leisure. Without haste
Wrth fy modd	I am delighted
Wn i ddim	I don't know
Wyneb i waered	Upside down. Face downwards
Ych a fi!	Ugh!
Y dydd o'r blaen	The other day
Y rhan fwya	Most. Majority

Y tro nesa	*Next time*
Y tro diwetha	*The last time*
Yma ag acw	*Here and there*
Ymhen awr	*In an hour's time*
Ymhell	*Far*
Ymhlith	*Among*
Yn bendramwnwgl	*Headlong*
Ynghau. Ar gau	*Shut*
Yn llygad ei le	*Dead right*
Yn ôl ag ymlaen	*To and fro*
Yn rhy fuan	*Too early. Too quick(ly)*
Yn rhy hwyr	*Too late*
Yn wir	*Indeed*
Yn y bore bach	*In the early morning*
Yn ystod	*During*
Ysgwyd llaw	*To shake hands*
Yr un	*The same, each*
Yr un lle	*The same place*
Ceiniog yr un	*A penny each*